LIFE BALANCE
THE SUFI WAY

AZIM JAMAL &
NIDO QUBEIN

JAICO PUBLISHING HOUSE

Ahmedabad Bangalore Bhopal Chennai
Delhi Hyderabad Kolkata Mumbai

Published by Jaico Publishing House
121 Mahatma Gandhi Road
Mumbai - 400 001
jaicopub@vsnl.com
www.jaicobooks.com

© Azim Jamal & Nido Qubein

Published in arrangement with
Azim Jamal
10151 Gilmore Crescent
Richmond, BC, Canada, V6X 1X1

LIFE BALANCE THE SUFI WAY
ISBN 978-81-7992-677-2

First Jaico Impression: 2007
Second Jaico Impression: 2008

Printed by Pashupati Printers (P) Ltd., Delhi-95

CONTENTS

▨ CHAPTER 2
LIVING AND WORKING WITH PURPOSE   22-51

▨ CHAPTER 3
DISPLAYING POSITIVE PRIDE, NOT EGO   **52-73**

▣ CHAPTER 6
HAVING A SENSE OF CONTRIBUTING   130-154

▓ CHAPTER 7
ADOPTING WELL-BALANCED HEALTH   155-172

▓ CHAPTER 8
UNDERSTANDING THE TIME MYTH   173-195

▣ CHAPTER 9
PRACTICING ENLIGHTENED PERSISTENCE 196-215

▣ CHAPTER 10
MASTERING THE BALANCING ACT   216-249

▨ APPENDIX A

AUTHORS' JOURNEYS:
LIFE BALANCE LESSONS

▣ APPENDIX B

PREFACE

Most people lead lives that are out of balance. That's not surprising. We live in a frantic and stressful age in which change is the norm and stability is an endangered commodity. Though balance is needed to negotiate the bewildering situations that confront us, our equilibrium is constantly being challenged by the swirl of events. It's as if were living constantly in the eye of a whirlwind.

The age of communication only complicates matters. Hundreds of daily e-mails, cell phone calls, pager messages, faxes, and seemingly interminable meetings interrupt our concentration.

It doesn't have to be that way.

You can choose to lead a balanced life. It isn't your circumstances that bring imbalance to your life; it's the choices you make in response to them.

"Circumstances do not make you; they reveal you," wrote author James Allen in his book, "As a Man Thinketh."

Your choices create your destiny, and you are their master. You can choose to live a life in balance, or you can reel through this existence constantly off-balance.

The authors have interviewed busy people to learn what concerns them as they take on the responsibilities of home and career.

HERE ARE SOME OF THE LAMENTS WE'VE HEARD:

▨ It's impossible to be a successful executive and be a loving and contributing family member. We must choose one or the other.

▨ Most of us are caught in an activity trap. We're too busy to give our children the nurturing they need, resulting in insecurity that leads to emotional issues later in their lives. They resort to quick-fix solutions such as alcohol and drugs to avoid pain. This just perpetuates the problem.

▨ Executives keep busy at work to avoid the realities at home.

▨ People live fearful lives, having lost all means of real communication with the people close to them.

▨ We are making a living but are ruining our lives. We continue to do work we don't like because we have no choice.

▨ People are beginning to live secret lives and to avoid authenticity.

▨ As we struggle with large mortgages and other debts, we find it more advisable to conform than to take risks, especially when we're getting older.

▨ Business organizations have no souls.

▨ Business has lost its meaning; it's just profit-making for the sake of profit-making.

■ We are being squeezed like lemons, and when the juice is gone we're discarded and replaced by fresh lemons.

■ There is no loyalty. We're just commodities, to be dispensed with when newer, more vital, more productive commodities come along.

■ People are in denial about their lack of balance. They avoid facing up to reality because reality is too painful.

■ We can either focus on one thing and excel, or strive for balance and forget about excellence.

Each of these dreary situations arises from a life out of balance. This book is designed to help you restore the balance.

Executives who find that the higher they climb on the corporate ladder the harder it is to maintain balance in their personal lives will learn how to keep their equilibrium and their success. They will learn how to make choices that lead to fulfillment in all facets of their lives.

If you're being thrown off balance by the stresses of a young family – running a taxi service to soccer games, dance classes, and music classes; taking part in the P-TA; providing food service, laundry, and housekeeping for your brood while trying to get ahead in your career and squeezing in a little quality time for yourself – you'll learn how to stay on your feet and enjoy the experience.

If you are part of the "sandwich generation," with responsibilities for children and elderly parents, you'll learn how to balance these responsibilities without being floored by your obligations.

HOW DO WE KNOW?

Because both of us have been there. We've brought balance into our lives by practicing the principles we enumerate in this book. Furthermore, as consultants, we have helped thousands of people from varying backgrounds, education, and cultures to live balanced lives.

Both of us were born in the East – Azim in East Africa and Nido in the Middle East – and have spent our professional lives in the West. We became successful using the best of Eastern and Western philosophies. We see the strengths and weaknesses in both, and in *Life Balance Is Your Choice,* we bring readers the best of both worlds.

Eastern philosophies, emphasizing reflection, silence, and going with the flow, are interwoven with the Western ideas of excellence, efficiency, effectiveness, and living and working to one's full potential. When we talk about the East and West, we are not talking about religious values, but the cultural, spiritual and ethical ones.

We have integrated East and West in our lives in a seamless way, and have sought to integrate them seamlessly into the book, so that the reader will be unable to distinguish ideas of Eastern origin from ideas of Western origin.

ABOUT THE AUTHORS

▧ Azim Jamal

A native of Tanzania in East Africa, educated in Great Britain and Canada, Azim Jamal married a girl from India. His parents, who are totally Eastern, and his children, who are totally Western, all live with him. Azim lives and breathes the balance between East and West.

Azim has volunteered 15 hours per week for 20 years to service to his fellow humans. He has provided service to Afghan refugees overseas. He has earned three professional accounting and financial degrees, and has been a senior partner in an accounting firm for 15 years.

He has spoken about Life Balance to more than a million people on five continents. He spends the hour between 4 a.m. and 5 a.m. daily in meditation, and has been doing so for 30 years.

Active in sports, Azim was named Sportsman of the Year locally both in Canada and in Tanzania. He brings the integration of his business, family, sports, and volunteer work as well as his Eastern and Western background into his speaking, consulting, and writing career.

▣ Nido R. Qubein

Nido arrived in America at the age of 17, with just a few dollars in his pocket and no knowledge of English. He is now an internationally acclaimed recognized educator, professional speaker, consultant, and author. Nido has established a balance in his business, family and philanthropic pursuits.

In 2004, he was named president of his alma mater, High Point University, a highly respected academic institution with more than 3,000 undergraduate and graduate students from 34 countries and 36 American states. He is also the chairman of Great Harvest Bread Co., with 210 stores in 39 states. He is a corporate director of BB&T, America's 10th largest financial institution, with more than $100 billion in assets. He is CEO of an international management and consulting firm, chairman of a public-relations and advertising firm, and chairman of a regional business-magazine publishing company.

As a public speaker, he has headed the National Speakers Association and founded the National Speakers Association Foundation. He has been inducted into the Speakers Hall of Fame and the International Sales and Marketing Hall of Achievement. His public speaking has earned him the Cavett Award, the Master of Influence, and the Golden Gavel Award. As a proud American by choice and conviction, he takes particular pleasure in holding the Ellis Island Medal of Honor.

His philanthropic pursuits include the founding of the Nido Qubein Associates Scholarship Fund, which has provided 600 scholarships, worth almost $3 million, for deserving young people.

GUIDELINES FOR A BALANCED LIFE

We do not claim that achieving Life Balance will be easy, or that all imbalance will disappear from your life after you've read this book. But we do believe that you will be better equipped to achieve a balanced life in an effective and integrated manner if you follow our guidelines. This in turn can lead to a more meaningful and productive life for you.

We are proud to share this book with you and know that you will profit from reading it and applying its suggestions.

We wish you an integrated and well-balanced life.

Nido and Azim

INTRODUCTION

You are the master of your destiny. Your life, your freedom, your choices, are all in your hands. You become the master when you believe in yourself. Belief in self gives you power over your fate, and only you can bestow that belief. If you don't believe in yourself, no one else will.

Acting on that belief brings your dreams to your doorstep. Make them big dreams. If you think small, you remain small. What the mind conceives, the mind achieves. If you go to the ocean with one small bucket, the ocean will give you only one small bucket of water. If you go to the ocean with 1,000 buckets, the ocean will give you 1,000 buckets of water. What you believe and ask for you invite into your life. When you believe in yourself, the whole world begins to believe in you.

Do you feel overworked and underutilized? Maybe it's because you have not discovered your purpose or calling in life. You have not found a cause larger than yourself to become involved in. You have not understood the magic of Life Balance – the synergy of your body, mind, and soul. Life Balance encapsulates purposeful living and the bounty of giving.

When you focus on your calling in life and on making a difference, you unleash your potential.

What does Life Balance mean? Why do we need it? And how can we find it? Let's look for some answers.

THE MEANING OF LIFE BALANCE

Achieving a balanced life means setting priorities: understanding what is important and making time for it. It means being in control of your choices rather than feeling controlled. It means realizing that the shape and structure of your life is ultimately in your hands, and does not depend on circumstances. It means knowing that you have a body, a mind and a soul, and thus that you have physical, mental, emotional, and spiritual needs. It begins by recognizing the areas in your life that have been neglected and need attention.

Life Balance can be viewed in many ways. It can be a balance between home and work. It can be a state of balance in one's physical, mental, emotional, financial, and spiritual health.

When you are in Life Balance, you are able to spend sufficient time, both qualitatively and quantitatively, in areas that you have defined as important to you. Life Balance is a state of feeling and being. You know intuitively that you are doing the right things, and you're able to navigate through the many opportunities and challenges. You know what is important to you and you are able to choose appropriately.

Life Balance is not a static condition. It is a dynamic and evolving blend of the body, mind, and spirit.

To know what Life Balance means to you, it's essential to know what areas of your life are the most important to you.

We believe that your life is balanced when you are centered. Being centered allows you to find equilibrium amid flux and change.

You are centered when you have a set of principles that are well grounded. When you're centered, you know what you want and why you want it. This comes from clarity of purpose. This clarity allows you to navigate through changes without compromising your core values and principles. You become like an orchestra. It has diverse players and different instruments, yet all are synchronized to produce a beautiful symphony. This is how you synchronize your body, mind, and spirit to your purpose. You are able to make life decisions from your core values and principles, rather than succumbing to a reactive, "firefighting" mode.

Being balanced also means catering to your own needs as well as those of your family and the society you live in. You become an asset to the world you live in.

In one of his interviews, Nido was asked: "How do you define success?"

His response: "I define it in one word. That word is *balance*. When you are spiritually, mentally, physically, socially, and economically balanced, then you're a successful person. I'm focused on maintaining a balanced perspective in my life. I want to be intellectually growing. I want to be socially interactive. I want to be economically independent and progressive. I want to be spiritually growing. I want to be physically fit. You can't just focus on work, although work is very important. You have to focus on all of the things that in unison can lead to good things."

WHY YOU NEED LIFE BALANCE

You need Life Balance for at least six reasons:

⊠ 1. Life Balance will enable you to avoid burn-out, and it can sustain your success.

Real success is long-term, and you can sustain it without sacrificing your health, your relationships, and other important things in your life. If your efforts to succeed have left you burned out or have destroyed your physical health, you've paid a heavy price, and you really haven't achieved success.

The cost of job stress in the United States is estimated at well over $100 billion annually. Statistics Canada has estimated that about $400 billion in Canadian money (US$340 billion) has been spent on stress-related illness in the work place. In many cases, stress comes about because of a lack of balance. Success in one part of life is achieved at the expense of success in another. That's usually a bad tradeoff.

If you acquire billions of dollars but lose your health in the process, your money may enable you to afford the best medical treatment, but it won't compensate for your lost health.

If acquiring money has caused you to lose the love of family and friends, your financial wealth comes at a very high price. In the words of a country-western song out of the 1950s: "Money can't buy back your youth when you're old, or friends when you're lonely, or a love that's grown cold."[1]

Og Mandino put it aptly: "When all is said and done, success without happiness is the worst kind of failure."

---

[1] "A Satisfied Mind". song by Red Hayes and Jack Rhodes, Starrite.

You don't want to be alone when you get to the top of the mountain. Life Balance enables you to share your successes with your loved ones.

If your financial ambition causes you to lose connection with your spirituality, any success will come at the sacrifice of Life Balance. When your life is in balance, you treat home and work as friends, not enemies. You realize that work is a noble thing and provides the financial stability your home needs.

▨ 2. Life Balance creates synergy.

An active and healthy body helps the mind as well as the spirit. When your mind is active and positive, it helps your body and your spirit. And when your soul is nourished, it helps your body and your mind. The synergistic effect that occurs through balance results in all-round productivity. A healthy body makes you feel energetic. When you are energetic your mind is alert and sharp. When your mind and body are active and sharp, you feel alert and focused, and this helps your concentration and reflection, which nourish your spirituality. When your soul is nourished with prayers and meditation, you feel good from within, and this creates peace of mind. When your mind and soul are peaceful and happy, you feel like exercising and keeping healthy.

▨ 3. Life Balance enables you to move from success to significance.

If success is your only aim, it is limited and does not create significance. You move toward significance when you use your success to make a difference and contribute to worthwhile causes.

Balanced living allows you to be *selfish* and *selfless* – selfish in the sense of catering to your own needs first; selfless in the sense that by catering to your own needs, you can be of help to others. When you use your life to serve others and contribute to good causes, you move from success to significance.

▣ 4. Life Balance enables you to find meaning and fulfillment.

When you spend enough time, and spend it well, in areas that are important to you, and when you contribute your talents and resources toward the good of humankind, the result is immense satisfaction with your life. You will find meaning, fulfillment and happiness.

▣ 5. Life Balance enables you to unleash your potential.

When your life is balanced, you have a far greater chance to live up to your potential. Through synergy, significance and sustainability, you tap into your reserve and go farther and longer.

▣ 6. Life Balance enables you to have impact on the world.

The world is made up of more than 200 countries and dependent territories. These in turn are divided into states, provinces and other political subdivisions. But the basic unit for all of human society is the family. And families are made up of individuals. So every individual who is balanced and is making a contribution toward others is making a difference in his country and, eventually, the world.

We're not exaggerating when we say that our actions affect the globe, and the actions of individuals in other parts of the globe affect us. The reality is that we are living in a global village, in which everything that happens has a global impact. We can learn from one another, and we can use what we learn to benefit everyone.

LIFE BALANCE: A MATTER OF CHOICES

You can do almost anything in life but not everything. When two desirable values contradict each other, it's necessary to strike a balance.

Meritocracy, effectiveness, and efficiency are valuable qualities. But what do you do when they clash with pluralism, diversity, principles and values? You strike a balance.

Caring for those less fortunate than you is an admirable trait. But what do you do when meeting another's needs would put you flat on your back? Remember the flight attendant's pre-takeoff instructions: Put the oxygen mask over your own face first; then you won't pass out while you're putting it over the face of the other person. If you're flat on your back, you can't help anyone.

We all want to put aside something to pass on to our children and grandchildren. But what if maintaining our own well-being requires all the resources we can muster? Care first for yourself. Otherwise, you may become a burden to your children before you can pass anything on to them.

You can think of many other choices: between self-interest and service to your country; between economic prosperity and preservation of the environment; between candor and honesty and concern for the feelings of others; between enjoying life to the full limits of your income and putting aside funds for your retirement years.

How can you make those choices?

You do it the same way you make choices between what you want in a house or car and what you can afford.

Do you really need a marble foyer, or would hardwood and an Oriental rug do the trick? Do you want double-paned insulated windows, or would you rather save that money and put it into a finished basement?

Do you need a 7-liter, 400-horsepower V-8, or would a 250 hp V6 serve as well? It may depend on whether you value fuel economy or fast acceleration. Do you want a sporty coupe, a roomy sedan, or a spacious, go-anywhere SUV? Each of these vehicles will do things the others won't do. None of them will do everything you might want it to do. You have to decide which capability is the most desirable or practical for you.

Life is a series of balancing acts. You have to make choices of what to do and what not to do. You have to pick up some things you desire and drop others.

In this book, we're going to learn how to become aware of the choices we must make. Then we'll learn to make those choices consciously until we achieve mastery. After that, appropriate choices will come natural to us.

CHAPTER 1

INVITING BALANCE AMID CHANGE

> **W**e live in a moment of history where change is so speeded up that we begin to see the present only when it is already disappearing.
>
> — R.D. Laing

QUESTIONS TO PONDER:

- Are you equipped to handle change?
- Have you ever had to fight change? What was the experience like?
- Are you fearful of change? How can you harness that fear?
- Do you embrace change naturally? Are you adaptable, fluid, and flexible?
- Do you keep your principles intact amid change?
- Do you choose your own change proactively, or are you always reacting to change?
- Do you have the courage to change when it is in your interest to do so?
- What changes have you experienced in your life, and what did they do to you?

▧ Can you recall the positive consequences that change brought?

CHANGE IS COMING: COUNT ON IT

Life isn't static; the one thing you can count on is change. Change can be positive or it can be negative. It can be a refreshing stimulant or it can also be a destructive enemy of balance and harmony.

As Nido wrote in his book, *The Time Is Now, the Person Is You:*

To many people, change is more threatening than challenging. They see it as the destroyer of what is familiar and comfortable rather than the creator of what is new and exciting.[2] ▧

To make sure that change doesn't sweep away all that is valuable to us, we must maintain equilibrium. Having equilibrium in a state of constant change is what Life Balance is all about.

For confident people, change is opportunity. They're willing to venture out of their comfort zones to embrace change and use it to their advantage.

For timid people, change is daunting. They prefer to remain in their comfort zones, content with mediocrity, preferring comfort to excellence. They choose the security of the familiar over the challenge of the unknown.

Change becomes exciting when you choose it yourself. Then it's not an unwelcome threat but a welcome adventure. Chosen change bolsters your resilience. It enables you to adjust to new

---

[2] ▧ Nido Qubein, The Time is Now, the Person Is You
(High Point, N.C.: Executive Press, 1997) p. 23

circumstances and bounce back from adverse developments.

You'll find change easier to handle if you arm yourself with a positive attitude and involve yourself in a strong and supportive social network.

Change, if viewed as a positive step toward growth and opportunity, can invite balance. But change, if mishandled, can result in imbalance. In this chapter, we'll discuss some constructive responses to change.

CHANGE IS A CONSTANT PHENOMENON

It has been said that you can't step in the same river twice because the river is constantly flowing. The same is true of time. Time flows in a continuum of change.

Our age is marked by accelerated human evolution. New patterns are replacing old ones very rapidly. Consider how the Internet and other technologies have revolutionized the way you communicate and do business, or how the events of 9/11 have altered your perception of the world.

In today's global environment, rapid change makes balance difficult. We have to learn and relearn even as technological advances confront us with the threat of information overload.

CHANGE BRINGS STRESS

Stress is one of the weapons change uses to throw us off balance. According to the Occupational Health and Safety News and the National Council on Compensation Insurance (U.S.A.), in a recent year:

▨ Up to 90% of all visits to primary-care physicians were for stress-related complaints.

🔲 More than 50% of lost workdays were stress-related, which means that stress was keeping about a million people per day from attending work.

One survey by the Journal of Occupational and Environmental Medicine found that:

🔲 Health care expenditures were nearly 50% greater for workers who reported high levels of stress.

According to the American Institute of Stress:

🔲 40% of job turnover was due to stress.

A report by StatsCan, Conference Board & Catalyst, showed that:

🔲 57 % of Canadian women 15 years and older had jobs, compared to 24% in 1951.

🔲 63 % of mothers with children under 3 worked, up from 28% in 1976.

🔲 75 % of female executives believed commitment to family hindered advancement; 41% delayed or skipped having children.

🔲 91 minutes was the average time devoted to a child under 5 each day by a mother in a two-income family. A father in a similar household devoted, on average, just 47 minutes a day.

According to Holmes/Rahe, inventors of the now-famous stress scale that rates life-change units, life was 44 per cent more difficult in the first decade of the 21st century than it was 50 years earlier. Most children experienced less change 50 years ago, so most people who grew up in that less frenetic era need to adjust their attitude toward change.

CHANGE CAN ADVERSELY AFFECT BALANCE

If you let change stifle you or stagnate you, it will affect your self-esteem, your relationships, and eventually your health, throwing your life out of balance. You'll become like the ancient dinosaurs, well adapted to an old environment but unable to survive in a changed environment. And like the dinosaurs, you'll become extinct or out of place among those who have adapted.

STRATEGIES FOR CONSTRUCTIVE RESPONSES TO CHANGE

Here are some things you can do to respond constructively to change:

▨ Become adaptable.

▨ Embrace change. View it as an opportunity for growth.

▨ Anticipate change.

▨ Use your repositories of problem-solving and coping strategies when faced with changes in your life.

▨ Use major crises to create breakthroughs.

▨ Engage in lifelong learning to stay abreast of change.

▨ Keep your principles intact despite change.

▨ Use change to break bad patterns.

▨ Grow from your experiences of changing circumstances.

▨ Realize the rewards that come with change.

▨ Connect with our spirituality.

5

ADAPTABILITY LEADS TO BALANCE

Nido and Azim both prospered because they were able to adapt to dramatic changes in their cultural surroundings. Both moved from the East to the West, Nido arriving in the United States and Azim migrating to the United Kingdom. Both moved at age 17. Each had to struggle early on in adapting to his new homeland. Growth from boyhood to manhood was rapid; they had to be on their feet quickly to meet the challenges and take advantage of the equally abundant opportunities. They saw clearly that the West held many good things for them that were not available in the East. They also realized that the East offered some assets that the West did not offer. They were able to focus on the best of both worlds. Their journeys are summarized in Appendix A.

PEOPLE ARE IN LOVE WITH CHANGE

Conventional wisdom holds that people dislike change. That's a myth. People love to change their clothes, their hairstyles, and their jobs. They're excited by new offices. They love to rearrange furniture. In our day and age, unfortunately, people regularly change marriage partners and in other ways rearrange their lives. Our physical bodies are constantly changing, and the physical environment is, too. Our minds are also changing. People don't dislike change; they're in love with it.

Technological progress has turned change into an irresistible force. Some people respond by trying to turn themselves into immovable objects. And as Fred Astair sang in one of his memorable movies, when an irresistible force meets an immovable object, "Something's gotta give."

Change may be inevitable, but you needn't allow it to sweep you away. Suppose you were to fall out of a boat in the middle of a swift-flowing river. Would you try to swim upstream to get back to the place where you fell out? Not if you wanted to survive. Instead, you would swim downstream, with the current, gradually moving closer to the shore. The current could even be your ally, sweeping you closer to shore as it approached a bend in the river.

The same strategy will work for you in negotiating the river of change. You won't be able to return to the conditions that existed in the past. But you can exert influence over the conditions you'll encounter in the future, and you can even use the forces of change to take you where you want to go with your life. The key is to remain fluid in the face of change. If you remain rigid, you'll break.

People used to dream about a golden age of leisure when machines would take over the work of humans, leaving us with time on our hands that we could spend any way we liked.

That was just a dream. Technological changes have brought longer working days for most people in the hi-tech sector. The eight-hour work day is a thing of the past. Work days of 11 to 12 hours are no longer the exclusive burden of top executives; they have become the norm for many down in the ranks.

Longer hours on the job make it increasingly difficult to balance time between work and family. Some companies have addressed this situation by making working hours more flexible, providing day care for employees' children, and allowing staff members to work from home.

Susan, a friend of ours, has young children and an aging mother. She has had to adjust her work hours to play the role of both child and mother. That meant working fewer hours and earning less income. Sometimes you have to make hard choices to achieve balance. But she made that choice and was happy to do so. Meeting the needs of her mother and children gave her a good feeling, and that good feeling stimulated her creativity. She made up for some of her lost salary by devising better investment strategies and reducing her tax liability.

When you use change to promote growth, you become adaptive. Adaptive people have a basic trust of the world. They assume that new situations or new people pose no threat, and they act on their assumptions until they're proved wrong. They are also good at adapting in different ways to different situations. That may be the most logical thing to do, but it's not always the most obvious. They have learned to balance life in the face of constant change.

INVITE LIFE BALANCE BY EMBRACING CHANGE

Thomas Watson's circumstances were dramatically changed after he was fired from a good job at National Cash Register – now NCR. He didn't let that throw him off balance. Instead, he founded his own company, International Business Machines. We now know it as IBM. And we now know Tom Watson as one of the legends of the business world.

When Lee Iacocca had differences with Henry Ford II, the automotive scion reminded the president of his largest division that the name on the building was Ford, not Iacocca. Iacocca was out of a job. The ousted executive didn't mope. He took over the presidency of the floundering Chrysler Corp., put it back on its feet, and made a handsome fortune for himself.

Both Watson and Iacocca refused to be swept away by change. Instead, they let change sweep them to success.

When you embrace change, it loses its sting. You diffuse relieve the tension, and it becomes part of your life – something you can manage. You then welcome the change and look forward to it and use it to your own advantage.

As you experience and learn, you grow. And, as you grow, your sensitivity to certain things is lessened. Fear, for instance, dwindles at each successive level of growth. You become able to enjoy more with less effort, and things that looked like major hurdles are now inconsequential bumps.

Without experience, you'll always be a rookie in life. A super hockey player, for instance, becomes really great only after years of experience at playing the game in a highly competitive league. A wonderful speaker becomes world class only after successfully delivering several hundred speeches. Experience gives you the knowledge, understanding, and wisdom to succeed. You know where the pitfalls are and what mistakes not to repeat. You become mature and eventually achieve conviction.

ANTICIPATE CHANGE

"Any change, even a change for the better, is always accompanied by drawbacks and discomforts," wrote British author Arnold Bennett.

That means that stress always accompanies change, but there are ways to deal with it. The best way to is to anticipate change and get ready for it. If you know you're going from a warm building into the frigid outdoors, you put on a warm coat and gloves, and the temperature change doesn't shock you. If you know you're about to hit a bump in the road, you brace yourself, and you don't get thrown from your seat. It's only when you get caught off guard that you get into trouble. So be alert for change. If you're complacent, you will probably miss the signs that it's coming your way.

"Change descends on every one equally," said Azim Premji, CEO of Wipro Corporation of India. "It is just that some realize it faster."

While sudden changes get attention because they are dramatic, it is the gradual changes that are ignored until it is too late, as illustrated in the story of the boiled frog. If you place a frog in a pot of water and suddenly increase the temperature, the frog will notice and quickly jump out if it can. But if the temperature is very slowly increased, one degree at a time, the frog does not realize it until it boils to death.

You must develop your own early-warning system for change. If you anticipate change and stay alert for its first signs, you can position yourself to take advantage of it.

To deal effectively with change, you must keep up with changes. You can't adjust to what you don't know. Read extensively the literature dealing with the field in which you pursue success. Look for the trends and develop strategies for riding these trends to success.

Don't overlook the possibility of influencing change. Nido puts it this way:

Are you a thermometer or a thermostat? A thermometer only reflects the temperature of its environment, adjusting to the situation. But a thermostat initiates action to change the temperature in its environment.[3]■

PROBLEM-SOLVING AND COPING STRATEGIES

We cope with change by using our repositories of problem-solving and coping strategies. All of us have in reserve enormous potential for coping with different situations. When changes confront us, we can tap into those repositories and draw upon an array of trouble-shooting methods and coping strategies. But if we're not exposed to change, those talents remain untapped.

Growing up conditions us to normal change. We see infants grow into adolescence, then into adulthood. We see the barren limbs of winter sprout spring leaves, then burst into blossoms that mature into summer fruit. We see the fall foliage grow dull and recede once more into the barrenness of winter. As the birthdays pile up, we encounter sickness and death among our loved ones and quietly accept the fact that one day they'll claim us too. These changes

---

[3]■ Nido Qubein, The Time Is Now, the Person Is You. (High Point, N.C.: Executive Press, 1997), p. 23.

are a part of our normal existence, and normal people learn to cope with them.

But when a 9-11 disaster comes along, or economic depression, or crime and violence that touch close to home, we need to tap into our repositories of coping strategies.

Azim's friend Anna found a way of coping after cancer took her husband from her. She decided to visit sick people in the hospital twice a week as a way of giving back something to people who were sick and lonely. She regards these comforting visits to the sick as a gift to her husband.

The most positive approaches for getting through life-changing events are drawn from our repositories of problem-solving behavior and coping strategies. We accumulate these mechanisms simply by living and coping. They are there to draw upon when change falls heavily on our lives.

USE MAJOR CRISES TO CREATE BREAK-THROUGHS

People adapt to change in different ways. That's OK. You may decide to profit from the experiences of others who have coped successfully with disruptive change. This may enable you to avoid the mistakes they made and to emulate their successes. But if you have different methods that work for you, that's just as good.

Whether you realize it or not, you are multi-faceted. You have immense inner resources you may not be aware of until you need them. You play the survival game day by day, and these challenges build up your resources as surely and as unconsciously as physical work builds up body muscles. When crisis strikes, these emotional muscles are there to be put to use.

Change can be life-transforming in a positive way if you embrace it wholeheartedly. But the embrace can't be tentative. You must be willing to make the change as permanent as the change that turns a caterpillar into a butterfly.

The caterpillar goes into a cocoon thinking it's the end of its existence. But in reality it's preparing for a new beginning as a totally different creature: a butterfly. Change is necessary for this marvelous metamorphosis. In our lives, too, drastic change or major crises are sometimes necessary to create breakthroughs that bring about transformation.

So make a clean break with the past. It can be scary, but it is also wonderfully rewarding. Don't be like some pilots who have died because they stayed with their disabled aircraft too long. They preferred the familiarity of the cockpit to the unfamiliarity of the parachute, even though the cockpit had become a death trap and the parachute was their ticket to safety.

INVITE LIFE BALANCE BY PURSUING LIFELONG LEARNING

Lifelong learning is the key to adapting to change. When you master the skills required to meet the changing demands, you acquire confidence in facing change. You learn from every experience. So be attentive and open to learning. Enhancing your skills and education will make you creative and will help you achieve Life Balance.

Gerry, a client of Azim's, was almost fired as an architect. A partner in his firm told him that he did not have what it took to be an architect. He negotiated a three-month grace period. If he failed to prove his worth during this period, he would be fired. Gerry proved his worth so convincingly that he not only retained his job but was also eventually offered a partnership in the business. How did this turnaround happen? Gerry was open to the feedback, engaged in improving his weaknesses, and believed in his own capacity to excel. The effort Gerry made enabled him to move forward to better opportunities. It improved his chances of inviting success and Life Balance.

When change is hard and puts you to the test, you may err sometimes. When that happens, let your sense of humor keep you going. Laughter can drain the hurt from your mistakes, and a sense of humor can make it easier to work on your shortcomings. If you can laugh as you remember the mistake, you'll be less likely to repeat it.

CHANGE YOUR HABITS, BUT NOT YOUR PRINCIPLES

"Only the wisest and stupidest of men never change," observed Confucius. He meant that the wisest men stick firmly to their principles whereas the stupidest of men stick to their old bad habits.

In the sea of change, your principles are the stabilizing anchors. They keep you steady while the world around you foams and froths, rocks and sways. In a changing landscape, they are the mountains of stability, standing upright and intact, like the Himalaya, the Andes, and the Rockies. In the tree of life, they are the roots that remain steadfast though the leaves change color and shed; though the sap recedes with the onset of cold.

When you experience change, stop and connect with the truth within you; become a catalyst and a transitional person. Principles are the fulcrum on which you create Life Balance. Principles remain unchanging and hold you at a steady equilibrium.

BUILD A SOLID BELIEF SYSTEM

"Be a servant of your conscience and a master of your will," wrote Dr. Marcus Bach, a leading authority on the world's religions and inter-cultural relations. That's good advice. To follow it, you'll need a solid belief system based on your principles.

Your belief system will provide you with a set of core values that mature with your experiences and knowledge. You may adjust your systems as you grow, holding onto precious values that retain meaning.

Occasionally, you must reassess values to see if those rules of old still fit your current situation. Old values keep you safe and get you started on the next leg of the journey. They also allow you to process information and categorize and file it away in your head. Such values keep you emotionally, mentally and physically strong. As you grow and mature, you can handle more of life. Then you have to assess old unnecessary rules and put new ones in place that allow you to move forward.

During change, you feel a fear of the unknown, because you're venturing outside safe and known limits. Your values and belief systems will keep you from feeling lost or unbalanced. You can overcome fear of change by accepting the fact that your beliefs might change over time, but that you can control the change so that it occurs at your pace. You sometimes need to readjust your values to achieve a fulfilling life.

BREAK THE PATTERN TO ACHIEVE BALANCE

In stable times, habitual patterns work for you. They become your preferred patterns of reacting. You take the same route to work every day. You don't have to map it out in your mind every morning. It's almost as if every turn were programmed into your car's steering. Taking that route is an involuntary choice.

When a new thoroughfare makes it easier and more convenient to take another route, you still find yourself habitually going the old way until you consciously establish a new pattern. For a while, you have to map out the new route mentally and force yourself to take it instead of the old route.

Change stops the process of involuntary actions. It breaks the pattern and demands that you respond appropriately. For many, this can cause stress. Medical experts tell us that stress is caused by the body's instinct to defend itself. The mind perceives change as a challenge and it gears up to meet it. If the challenge doesn't materialize, the body's engine continues to race, causing stress.

The best remedy for stress is to avoid the event that causes it. But this often is impossible. When you can't avoid stress, your best course is to change the way you react to it. Try to see change as a positive challenge, not a threat.

Another tactic is to find ways to take a break from the stress. Some people get relief through taking part in group sports. Others attend social events and pursue relaxing hobbies. This brings temporary respite from the stress. It isn't the load that does the damage; it's the length if time you carry it. If you're moving a stack of books from one corner of the room to the other, the load may seem light. But if you have to carry those books several blocks, you'll find them getting heavier by the second.

LET CHANGE BE A GROWTH AGENT

Maturity arrives through experience and not through revelations. Revelations make you dependent on others; life's lessons make you independent.

Sometimes, change needs both time and attention. If you don't allow it adequate time and focus, you won't be able to master the skills required to adapt and meet the change.

OVERCOMING THE CHALLENGE OF CHANGE

If you are faced with major change you can overcome it by:

▨ Developing skills and capacities for managing change and living in harmony with the environment.

▨ Developing positive and proactive ways of dealing with loss and of learning and growing through adversity.

▨ Keeping open lines of constructive communication and discovering and taking advantage of new opportunities through change.

Regardless of the situation, you can always adapt to new circumstances, becoming stronger and more knowledgeable for the changes. If hard times come, remember that they don't last forever, unless you allow them to. When encountering a rough patch, make plans to adjust for better times.

REAP THE REWARDS THAT COME WITH CHANGE

Recognizing the value in change can ease the trauma it causes. You can create a roadmap for the future by anticipating change and looking at the nature of the opportunity it provides. You can reassess your goals and expectations. You can display your leadership traits by helping others cope with change. You can maintain equilibrium amid change by keeping to your center.

Azim, while working for a major accounting firm, was nicely told to find a different job. He was told that the firm did not want to let him go, but this particular job was not his "cup of tea." So whenever he was ready to leave, he could leave. Azim gave his notice the next day. This gave Azim the impetus to complete his Certified General Accountants examination much quicker. He joined a well-established smaller firm and later became a senior partner in that firm. The flexibility acquired from working with the smaller firm enabled him to pursue other interests, including speaking and writing. He could not have pursued those interests while working with the larger firm, and an eventual partnership in that firm was only a distant dream.

Adjusting to change is like jumping into a pool of cold water. At first you feel shock and discomfort. But the longer you stay in, the more pleasant the new environment becomes. Once the body adjusts to the change in water temperature, you're ready to call out, "Come on in; the water's fine." In the same way, you'll adjust to new business and social environments and soon find them as comfortable as the old – and more stimulating.

CONNECT WITH YOUR SPIRITUALITY

Change is a way to grow physically, mentally, emotionally, and spiritually. When hardship and sorrow come, you connect with your spirit and dig for your faith. Dealing with the loss of a loved one is particularly difficult, because death makes us feel vulnerable. But death of a loved one can be turned into a very enriching experience if you go inward and connect with your spirituality. You can turn it around by getting involved in helping the less fortunate or by serving in causes your departed loved one was interested in.

When you have a strong, positive outlook on life, you can view change as a positive force in your life. You view it with a welcoming eye – as a blessing, even. You can view everything in life that way. Make it a habit to look at everything positively, including change.

DON'T JUST SIT THERE

It should be clear by now that you can't deal with change by sitting still. As the great humorist Will Rogers put it: "Even if you are on the right track, you'll get run over if you just sit there."

You'll find balance by becoming dynamic and fluid, and by cultivating the ability to navigate amid rapid change. The key is to hold on to your center, and to keep your feet firmly on the ground despite all the shaking above the floor. If you keep your principles firm, you can use them as your rudder. Take time to reflect; don't get trapped in the activity syndrome and in the busyness of life. Look at change as an opportunity for growth. By creating breakthroughs you can actually use change to your advantage.

SUMMARY

In summary, balance amid change takes place when you follow these guidelines:

▨ (1) Be adaptable to new circumstances and changes; don't resist them.

▨ (2) View change as a blessing for opportunity and growth.

▨ (3) Use your repositories of problem-solving and coping strategies when faced with changes in your life.

▨ (4) Look for opportunities to create break-throughs during major changes and crises.

▨ (5) Engage in lifelong learning to stay abreast of change.

▨ (6) Keep your principles intact despite change.

▨ (7) Use change to break bad patterns and grow from the experiences of change.

YOUR GOAL-SETTING EXERCISE

CHAPTER II: INVITING BALANCE AMID CHANGE

Which areas in your life do you need to work on to achieve Life Balance amid change? Ask yourself: "What is the one big obstacle getting in the way of my working and living a balanced life amid rapid change?" Set your goal and timeline to overcome this obstacle.

My goal is to work on the following areas in terms of maintaining balance amid rapid change:

....

....

....

I commit to the following timelines to implement this habit:

....

....

....

If I follow through with this goal it will make a significant difference in my balanced living.

GOAL-SETTING EXAMPLE

I will view the change of having a baby as a blessing and an opportunity. I will take six months off from work and subsequently reduce my work hours to 30 from 50 hours a week. I will use the time I am home to bond deeply with my child and to reflect on my new life as a parent.

> *It is not necessary to change. Survival is not mandatory.*
>
> – W. Edwards Deming

LIVING AND WORKING WITH PURPOSE

> Something opens our wings. Something makes boredom and heart disappear. Someone fills the cup in front of us. We taste only sacredness.
>
> – Rumi

QUESTIONS TO PONDER:

⊠ Do you know the meaning of a purposeful life, and do you stay in this big picture?

⊠ Do you have a clear, consistent and internalized blueprint for your life?

⊠ Do you live an *energetic* life?

⊠ Do you focus on your goals, or on your obstacles?

⊠ Do you compromise your values and principles in pursuit of your purpose?

⊠ Do you act on your dreams?

⊠ Are you living a *pretentious* life, or a purposeful and authentic one?

YOU ARE HERE FOR A REASON

You were born into this world for a reason. You are here for a nobler purpose than just to eat, sleep, produce offspring, and die. You are here to make a difference. You are here to shine your light and leave the world in better shape then you received it. You are here to display the gifts you have been blessed with. You are here to use those gifts to make a contribution and create significance.

There is no one like you in this world. No one in this world can match your smile, style, or DNA. No one in this world can speak like you or think like you. You are unique, gifted, and special. Your gifts are tied to your purpose. Discover them and use them fully. When you do things you were born to do and use your innate gifts to make a difference, you are living and working with purpose.

When you live with purpose, you are energized and focused, and have a sense of direction. Life Balance becomes easier, because you are concentrating on things that are important to you and not wasting time on unimportant things. Your life has meaning, direction, and focus, and you are able to pay attention to your work, family, and spirituality.

In this chapter we discuss the following:

▨ What a "purposeful life" looks like.

▨ Benefits to living a purposeful life, and how it helps Life Balance.

▨ Obstacles to living a purposeful life

▨ Strategies to overcome these obstacles

WHAT A PURPOSEFUL LIFE LOOKS LIKE

"When love and skill work together, expect a masterpiece," wrote John Ruskin, the Victorian artist, scientist, poet, environmentalist, and philosopher.

23

All of nature is on call, operating in silence and yet on purpose. The mighty oak was once a little nut that stood its ground. The acorn contains the design for the fully developed oak tree in all its mightiness. Where you find purpose and strong principles, there you find success and balance.

A ship would never sail without a destination. Similarly you can't find Life Balance without having a clear objective. When you have purpose, you know where you are going, and you know why you want to go there. You are driven to get there. A sense of purpose creates energy, meaning, gumption, and love. You lose track of time doing things that have a solid purpose. You find enjoyment and make a difference to others.

Finding Life Balance starts with having clarity of purpose — knowing what you want and why you want it. This applies to your work and to your home. Without clarity we are unable to focus. This leads us to do too much – maybe in too many directions – and results in imbalance. Remember, it is not how fast you go or how efficient you are that counts; it's whether you're going in the right direction. If you are heading in the wrong direction, even thinking positively will help only temporarily.

Purposeful living enables you to know what's really important in your life. Focusing on important things in life leads to balance. Focusing on unimportant things wastes time and energy and leads to imbalance.

You should not confuse important things with urgent things. In fact, there is an inverse relationship between what's urgent and what's important. What is important is generally not urgent. Things become urgent only if we have neglected to do them. Focusing on urgent things can lead to imbalance. Although many of us are aware of the differences between urgent and important, most of us are unaware of where our time disappears to. Awareness comes from keeping track of how we spend our time.

BENEFITS TO LIVING A PURPOSEFUL LIFE

"The more I want to get something done, the less I call it work," commented Richard Bach, author of the best-seller "Jonathan Livingston Seagull."

When you enjoy your work, you are more efficient and effective, and this helps you achieve Life Balance. When you get involved in the right kind of work, you take a big step toward acquiring a sense of purpose and living a good life. Doing what you love in a conducive environment invites passion and makes it easier to wield your talent with maximum effect. You understand the bigger purpose of your work. You're like the mason who knows that he is building a cathedral instead of just laying stones.

When you do purposeful work, you feel guided by principles. Your principles are the anchor, providing a source of steadiness amid tumultuous circumstances. If your anchor is bendable, then it will not hold the boat in place properly. In the words of Abraham Lincoln, "Important principles may and must be inflexible." If principles can be bent, they cannot serve as reliable guides to behavior.

"A musician must make music, an artist must paint, a poet must write if he is ultimately at peace with himself," said Abraham Maslow, a 20th-century American psychologist.

OBSTACLES TO LIVING A PURPOSEFUL LIFE

Few of us have personal direction early in life. Instead of choosing our own ideal jobs, we let the jobs choose us. Most jobs look great if you don't really know what you're looking for. If you haven't really decided where you want to go in your career, there are too many bewildering paths to take.

Many people seem to follow the same pattern in work or marriage: They leave a job that they've found unfulfilling and find the same kind of job next time around. The same applies for people who get divorced: They seem to end up marrying the same kind of person again. They then blame bad fortune and never realize that they simply didn't reflect long enough or deep enough to decide what sort of work they wanted or what sort of spouse best complemented them.

Take the example of Leslie, who works as an administrative assistant for an average-sized company. She doesn't like her job. She is interested in a job with more personal interaction. She finds her employer unreasonable and demanding. Every day she comes home miserable. This has affected her marriage and her relationship with her children. She has done this for 11 years. She is now 45 years old and feels that it is too late to change jobs.

It's not too late. She has to make the choice to live with purpose. That choice will exact a price in the short run, but she will be far better off in the long run.

She must begin by believing in herself, her attributes, and her gifts. She must identify what she loves to do and what her innate gifts are. If she has not been happy with her job, the chances are that she is part of the problem. She is probably not working at her optimum, and her attitude is not positive. This contributes to the flawed relationship with her employer and to her less-than-optimum performance. It is a lose-lose proposition. We could cite many examples of people caught in what seems for them to be no-choice situations.

Leslie can bring about a change in her life through lifelong learning, exploring options about her work and career, and discussions with her family about her dilemma.

"Successful and unsuccessful people do not vary greatly in their abilities," according to John Maxwell, leadership trainer and author of the book _Developing the Leader Within You._ "They vary in their desires to reach their potential."

STRATEGIES TO OVERCOME THESE OBSTACLES

Here are some ways to overcome obstacles to living a purposeful life at home and at work:

- Have clarity of purpose.
- Have a shared vision.
- Choose wisely to achieve Life Balance.
- Be willing to take risks.
- Eliminate doubt from your life.
- Seek authenticity, not charisma.
- Be transformational, not just transactional.
- Seek intentional congruence.
- Concentrate on being, not on doing.
- Close the gap between where you are and where you want to go.

CLARITY OF PURPOSE

"The sole purpose of education is to help you find out what you, with all your heart, must love to do," wrote Jiddu Krishnamurti, India-born 20th-century philosopher.

And American author Robert Byrne wrote that "The purpose of life is to live a life of purpose."

This wisdom from East and West boils down to this: To achieve a meaningful and significant life, you must have a vision, and a mission statement that tells how you expect to implement that vision.

That means you can't pick your line of work randomly. When making that choice, it's important to reflect, take a long look inside yourself, and answer some hard questions about who you are and what you want. The key to purpose lies within you.

The Sufis, a mystical branch of Islam, have a story about a man who lost his keys and searched for them in the street. A friend came by and helped him search. Finally, the friend asked, "Where were you when you lost your keys."

"In the house," replied the man.

"Then why aren't you looking for them in the house?" asked the friend.

"Because the light's better in the street," came the reply.

You have to look for the key to purpose where it lies – within you – and not where it's more convenient or less painful to look.

You can help identify your purpose by asking two questions:

▨ "If I were to die today, what would be written on my tombstone?"

▨ "If I had six months to live, how would I spend my remaining days?"

These questions put things in perspective. To answer them, you need to form a vision of what you want to be. You must identify your mission in life and describe that mission in a mission statement. At the end of this chapter, we'll guide you through the creation of one.

A mission statement can help you to remove the dust from the mirror so you can see clearly. You must separate truth and reality from the illusionary. You need a great deal of courage to challenge your beliefs and reach out to reality. If you are too caught up with the mundane, illusionary things of life, it will be difficult to get clarity.

Whenever you are confused about a course of action you need to take, you can go back to your mission statement and find the clarity of purpose there.

When you're guided by a vision and a mission statement, you no longer worry about whether you're ahead of or behind your neighbor. As Nido put it in his book, _The Time Is Now, the Person Is You_: "Winners compare their achievements with their goals, while losers compare their achievements with those of other people."[4]▨

When you are clear about your vision, and believe in your ability, you invite help from the Universe. A

---

[4]▨ Nido Qubein, The Time is Now, the Person Is You. (High Point, N. C.: Executive Press, 1997) P. 17.

thousand unseen hands come to your assistance. The universe conspires to help you.

So sing the song that you have come here to sing; do not just string and unstring your instrument. Work in areas of your calling. Keep your eye on your goal, and see how energized and motivated you become.

When considering a career you have to start by asking, "What are my strengths and weaknesses?" Once you have the answer, it will be easier to focus on your strengths and manage your weaknesses. According to the Buddhist tradition of the Right Livelihood, the right work would give you a chance to develop your abilities and overcome your own ego-centeredness. When you find yourself doing purposeful work, in your area of interest, it will energize you. Michael Jordan was a great basketball player, but he did not do nearly as well in baseball. Azim failed his high-school exams in science, but in accounting, he did better that anyone else in the history of the college.

Nido was asked in an interview: "What do you do best?"

His reply: "I am a critical thinker who helps my clients build transformational leadership in their organization. As a consultant, my strongest suit is to guide you through critical thinking to arrive at premises that are based in reason and on sound assumptions and therefore can help you build good strategies."

If you are not enjoying your work, you'll never become accomplished at what you do. Finding the right work comes from having both clarity of vision and clarity of mission. Developing mission statements both for your profession and for your family becomes crucial for clarity. Finding alignment between the two brings about congruence. A mission statement reveals the principles by which you would like to operate your life. It reflects your deep values and connects with your calling in life.

To help you achieve clarity, ask yourself the following:

▦ Do you know the one thing you *must* do?

▦ Are you spending your life stringing and unstringing the instrument instead of singing your song?

▦ Do you keep your eye on the goal or on the obstacles?

▦ Do you see and feel your goal and vision regularly?

▦ Is your work mission aligned to you personal mission?

▦ Do you know why you are doing what you are doing?

▦ Is your work your greatest delight?

▦ Does your purpose make a difference to others?

▦ Do you know that you are born with a mission to make a difference?

YOUR SHARED VISION

"The Passion of a shared vision empowers people to transcend beyond petty, negative interactions," according to Stephen Covey, author of *The 7 Habits of Highly Effective People*.

When you have a shared vision there is harmony among members of your work team and of your family team. You waste less time arguing about where you are going, and you tend to pull together toward your mutual goals. All this helps with balancing your life, because it saves time and energy.

You do not live on an island. You have needs and responsibilities outside yourself. Therefore, having a shared vision at home and at work makes a lot of sense, and increases your chances of success.

All family members need to buy into the vision. Everyone should be on board, showing mutual respect and a commitment to help one another achieve their individual goals. The same goes for your work team. Without involvement, team members will make no commitment.

It is said that people decide with their heads but commit from their hearts. The problem with most businesses is that they don't inspire much trust or commitment in the hearts of their employees because they don't let employees share a vision. CEOs and their employees have problems finding a common sense of purpose. Too often, there's little trust on either side.

Because they're working toward goals they feel no stake in, junior-level employees feel that they have no control over their jobs. Several research studies have proved that the mere feeling of having control over your day makes you healthier. This feeling of lack of power plays havoc with the health of junior employees.

If you are a leader in a corporation and would like better productivity from your team, your best bet is to encourage Life Balance for your team members. That means empowering them to capture their creativity, enabling them to perform better and for a longer duration.

Having a shared vision means that you are working with the following in mind:

▣ Being result oriented.

▣ Looking at the common ground and getting a buy-in from all stakeholders.

▣ Seeking commitment, which comes from involvement and understanding.

▣ Balancing the heart and mind. Involvement of heart brings commitment; involvement of mind helps with decisions.

▣ Thinking from the other person's viewpoint and developing a win-win attitude.

To help you achieve a shared vision ask yourself the following:

▣ Do I use the diverse strengths of all my team members to reach a common objective?

▣ Do I know which direction I'm going? Is my team working from the same map?

CHOOSE WISELY TO ACHIEVE LIFE BALANCE

People today are inundated with choices. They range from too many brands of cereal to too many career choices, to too many life choices. It all gets a bit overwhelming. The variables you deal with include where you will live and work and what's important for the family, for the children, and for you.

Choices create your destiny, and choices must be aligned with your mission in life. As you choose, so you become. Life Balance is a choice. You make choices daily, hourly, and monthly. When you choose appropriately – with wisdom, maturity, and clarity – you invite Life Balance.

When you choose to spend time with the family, you are choosing wisely and are inviting Life Balance. Azim recalls a dinner date he had with his daughter, Sahar, then 10 years old. As the dinner progressed, Azim was deeply moved (and even a little surprised) at how Sahar opened up and started to share of herself – her joys and her struggles. Azim was amazed at her candor and depth. In the intimate and honest connection they formed a good friendship. Azim felt he came to know his daughter on a deeper level.

When we spend time with our children, we build a powerful bond. Quality time is not enough; we also need to spend quantity time with them as well, especially when they are young. So the choices we make at home create balance or imbalance. The following tips are useful when making choices related to spending time with children:

- Speak at your child's level
- Reflect your child's feelings
- Have frequent family discussions
- Give your children lots of hugs

Making decisions about what you want in life means starting with yourself and not with the external demands of any situation. It's important to discover what is unique about yourself, what things in life really motivate you, and where your joy springs from. If your choices are based on these simple questions and you take time to reflect upon them – in solitude – your choices will be aligned with your priorities and will eventually invite Life Balance.

BE WILLING TO TAKE RISKS

If you want to live with purpose and thereby invite Life Balance, you must be willing to take risks. No objective worth pursuing comes without effort or risk. Those who strive and those who dare may be constantly tempted to return to their comfort zones. They must resist the temptation. A sense of perspective coupled with the ability to take risks when it matters is a powerful tool in constructing a meaningful life in the workplace. When you begin taking calculated risks that take you toward your objective, you feel more energetic and balanced. You foreclose the possibility that you will later find yourself saying, "If only I had taken that chance." This energy and balance also carry over into your personal life.

Most of the older people we've talked to agree that they've felt most alive when taking risks; that they felt a much greater intensity in their lives when trying new things and allowing themselves to learn, fail, try again, and continue to explore and learn.

This underscores the importance of seizing the moment; of reaching for the stars while you're gifted with youth, energy, and a sense of adventure. But your reach should not be blind. It must be guided by reflection and planning. Many of the seniors we've interviewed have told us they wished they had been more reflective in their prime. Many of them had been so caught up in the moment of action that they often lost focus on the meaning of what they were trying to accomplish.

Life moves at an ever-quickening pace, and by the time you've finished preparing and establishing yourself, its time to shift gears. Phase II, the second half of your life, has arrived, and the days, weeks, and years pick up speed like a river current approaching rapids. Suddenly your children are grown, your grandchildren are arriving, and you're the age your parents were when you first thought of them as "old." Time is suddenly the most precious currency in life, and you regret taking the risk-free course and holding back from doing the things you love doing.

Seek integrity not security. Integrity comes when you choose the work you love and are born to do.

ELIMINATE DOUBT FROM YOUR LIFE

To have doubts is to be human. But doubts are energy drains that bring on imbalance. They are stumbling blocks you need to clear out of your life.

Purposeful living at home and work leads to Life Balance. It's true that a degree of uncertainty keeps you from being careless; it's the thing that makes you suddenly remember that you haven't checked whether the stove was turned off or the doors were locked. A little uncertainty is OK if it keeps you on guard against dangerous situations.

If you nurture a strong sense of purpose, you'll be able to move forward and create your own vision for the future. Having a sense of purpose in your day-to-day life as well as for the overall future makes the difference between ability and inability to move toward greater fulfillment.

Some people allow themselves to feel like failures when they encounter obstacles to reaching their goals. Others treat the obstacles as temporary detours. They quickly find ways to return to the main road and continue toward their objectives. They never stop believing they'll get there. To them, one inch of doubt is too much. Never doubt your intentions or your desires. Have faith in the unknown and be your own biggest fan. When you believe in yourself, everyone else does too.

CONFIDENCE SERVED NIDO WELL

Nido came to America with no money, no knowledge of English, and no connections. He became successful because he did not doubt himself and his abilities. He saw America as the land of opportunity. If the streets were not paved with gold, they certainly were routes to riches for those willing to follow them with confidence. This was a land where, if he was willing to work hard enough and smart enough, he could make something valuable come of his life.

Nido, in his presentations, talks about the following key points that have an effect on purposeful living and working:

- Balance comes from authenticity, not charisma.
- Strive to be transformational, not transactional.
- Create intentional congruence.

BALANCE COMES FROM AUTHENTICITY, NOT FROM CHARISMA

Authenticity is significantly better than charisma. While being charismatic and dynamic are wonderful traits, being authentic is being precisely what the world perceives us to be. We can't fool people. They can see us coming a mile away.

All things begin with trust. When clients trust you, you can chart a course together for a better future.

Trust leads to reason. Wishing something were so doesn't make it so. So you have to work diligently at developing your critical thinking skills. Reason leads to focus. Focus is as important as intelligence, and the one choice you consistently make is whether you choose to be focused. Focus then leads to value, which is measured by the size of problems you can solve, and not by how much you get paid (although often the two are related). Value then leads to success, and success can lead to significance. Success is secular, and significance is spiritual, just as happiness is transient, but joy is lasting. Significance is influenced by passion, and passion is the result of purpose. *Being* leads to *doing*. It's not *I do and therefore I am;* It's *I am, and therefore I do*. Sounds heavy, but really it is a basic understanding about life and living and how work fits into all that.

Authenticity invites inner peace, which leads to balance. Authentic leaders aren't interested only in the fame or the money they gather, but genuinely desire to serve others through their leadership. Their interest lies in empowering the people they lead so that they can uplift their lives somehow. They are as guided by passion and compassion as they are by intellect and communication.

Conversely, some charismatic leaders – the most infamous examples being Adolph Hitler, Mussolini and, more recently, Saddam Hussein – are more driven by their megalomania or hunger for expression. Cults and gurus use guilt and fear to secure power over people and gain emotional control over their followers. People become too frightened or paranoid to leave these groups, which have often blinded them to reality until it is too late.

Authentic leaders know their strengths and weaknesses and are not afraid to be honest about both sides of their personalities. But charismatic leaders seek to hide their weaknesses behind their darker side. If you look back on your life, you'll probably find that the teachers who made school life more meaningful for you weren't necessarily the most knowledgeable instructors, but they were authentic people. They imparted a full sense of themselves and were able to transmit a more complete idea of humanity that made you want to be real and authentic too.

Authentic Leaders embody the values they advocate, and can model the new way of doing things. But the problem is that real transformational leaders are difficult to find. After they have reached satisfactory levels of power and influence, most leaders seem to lose their instincts to question and fire up people with principles and values. They don't really like the thought of risking their own stock options with major changes that the company may need. Is it understandable that seasoned directors, only a few years from retirement, will not be willing to take the same risks that got them their prominent positions in the first place?

If you want to be engaged in a more meaningful life, you have to transform your life by renewing your mind and linking to purpose. Authenticity linked to purpose creates synergy and meaning. On the other hand, Charisma, if it is charm without substance, can be problematic.

Azim was once asked to introduce a colleague at a seminar. Azim poured his heart out in the introduction. It was the kind of introduction that Azim would want someone to give him. The praise was authentic; the colleague's virtues were not exaggerated. The power of the introduction was heartfelt and sincere, and came with the right intention. When you give to others what you need most, your gift comes from the depth of authenticity and security. Azim admits that this has not always been easy for him to do.

When you practice authenticity in the family it is much more stable, happy, and balanced. The focus is on how you can support each other. There is no energy drain brought on by negativity and defense.

Authentic living means you are living in tune with your calling and your purpose. It means going to the source. It means no more lying to oneself. It means facing the truth and being aware.

As Azim puts it: "The whole world can think you are great, but if you do not feel that way from deep within, the world's opinion means little. What counts is being true to your deeper self, not to others' opinions about you."

BE TRANSFORMATIONAL, NOT TRANSACTIONAL

Nido encourages his clients to become transformational, not transactional. What's the difference?

To quote Nido:

Transactional leadership puts emphasis on what people do. Transformational leadership puts emphasis on what they become. Transactional leadership imparts a body of knowledge. Transformational leadership equips people to acquire knowledge on their own.

Transactional leaders focus on what they want to say; transformational leaders focus on the need to feel and believe.

Your beliefs lead to your behaviors, and your behaviors lead to results. It isn't what you and I say that matters; it's the effect it has long after we've said it. Transformational people recognize that it isn't something you do in front of your clients that impresses them; it's something you do *with* your clients. When clients "own" what you share and "invest" themselves in it, transformation is a likely result.

You feel it and hear it and see it when you have a transformational effect. Transactional people change behaviors; transformational people change hearts and minds. Transformational people are catalysts – they create positive change and grow exponentially.

Transformational people do things that have a lasting impact. They do not do things that are temporary and short-lived. They tend to build long-term relationships. They make huge changes, create great progress, and produce a metamorphosis through which the thing that is transformed becomes greater than its parts. They are like catapults.

Conversely, transactional people focus on the transaction – the give-and-take with a short-term outlook; the "You-scratch-my-back-and-I'll-scratch-yours" kind of attitude. They tend to make a lot of noise, but create only a splash. Transactional people drink beer, burp and then go to sleep. Anyone can do that. Transformation requires much more than that.

Howard Hughes and Elvis Presley are both examples of men who led lives of great accomplishment and reached great heights of fame and popularity, but died in misery amid all their wealth. Neither man appears to have gone beyond the pursuit of personal gratification to become a transformational force in the world.

Elvis left behind a great body of music and movies. He left his indelible stamp on generations of music. And he was known for random acts of generosity. Yet he never attempted to use his wealth and influence in a focused way to bring about a better world.

Howard Hughes had brilliant achievements in movie-making and in the aircraft industry, leaving behind such movies as "Hell's Angels," "Scarface," and "The Outlaw," and making genuine contributions to aircraft design and performance prior to World War II. But he spent his final years as an enigmatic recluse.

Hughes used his great wealth to pursue his personal interests. At the time of his death, his estate was valued at $2 billion, but his sole act of philanthropy was the founding of the Hughes Medical Institute. By turning over all of the stock of Hughes Aircraft Company to the institute, he made his billion-dollar-a-year weapons factory a tax-exempt charity. Since his death, the institute has become the nation's largest private source of support for biomedical research and science education. But it achieved that status almost by accident, and under the guidance of leaders who created a vision for it that went well beyond Hughes' dream of a tax shelter for his aircraft business.

Neither Presley nor Hughes seems to have followed a conscious purpose of fundamentally transforming their worlds. To do that, you must have a vision and believe in it, know your own inner guidance mechanisms, be grateful for your fortunes and privileges, and be open to receive the gifts of the universe.

Transformation comes about when you are purpose-centered and not ego-centered. A family that follows a "transformational outlook" has a far better chance of having lasting relationships than a family that follows a "transactional outlook."

CREATE INTENTIONAL CONGRUENCE

To be congruent means to be in agreement, to harmonize, or to correspond. When your life is in congruence, anything and everything you do is in harmony with your core values and principles. Intentional congruence means that you intentionally get involved in projects and associations that connect harmoniously with each other and with your overall core values and principles.

Intentional congruence is a purposeful system to maximize your potential through synergy, leverage, and interlocking opportunities. You know you have it when two or more of your activities and strategies cumulatively create more than either could create separately. Nido's network of interests provides a model. He is a professional speaker, which feeds into his consulting, which feeds into his magazine publishing, which leads to business for his public-relations firm. All of these create opportunities for the Great Harvest Bread Co., and add to his stature as the president of High Point University. Everything he does has an interlocking relationship with everything else he's involved in. The result is maximum effectiveness and productivity.

Living a life of congruence invites balance. Everything is connected to the bigger purpose. You can achieve that congruence by examining the purpose of your life and connecting everything you do to that purpose. Your purpose is at the center of your being and is the source of your security, guidance, and wisdom.

It is important, therefore, to determine what you want to place at the center of your being – what you want to become the source of your core motivation. The most stable and enduring source is a positive, well-thought-out set of principles by which you choose to live your life. Your principles are based on your values – the most important things in your life.

When your life is people-centered, the important thing to you is what others want. When it's possession-centered, the important thing is what you have. When it is activity-centered, the important thing is what you do. These are all external sources of motivation.

But when your life is principle-centered, the important thing is who and what you are. Your core motivation lies within you.

The principles we live by determine our character – the essence of who we are.

When you choose an external source of core motivation, you place yourself at the mercy of mood swings, inconsistent behavior, and uncontrollable changes of fortune. When you put principles at the center of your life, you have a solid, unwavering foundation for decision-making.

When we live by our principles, we are being true to ourselves. This is quite different from being self-centered. Self-centered people don't reach out to others, and don't concern themselves with others' interests. They therefore live their lives in emotional isolation, often developing mental-health problems.

By centering your life on valid principles, you create a stable, solid foundation for the development of your life-support factors. You embrace and encompass the truly important areas of your life. Successful relationships, achievement, and financial security will radiate from the principles at your core.

The principles you base your life on should be deep, fundamental truths, classic truths, or generic common denominators. They will become tightly interwoven themes running with exactness, consistency, beauty, and strength through the fabric of your life.

Intentions and desires come from your spiritual nature. Release them to the universe to take over, remembering that the universe knows more about you than you know about yourself. Surrender to its timing. Just as every seed embodies huge potential, so too does every person. Just as the seed must give itself to the fertile ground to reach its potential, so too must we give ourselves to the universe around us. The key is to marry the human mind with the universal mind and to become a conscious decision-maker.

When your inside and outside worlds are in harmony, you are enjoying intentional congruence.

LIFE BALANCE COMES FROM BEING, NOT DOING

During your work life, you've undoubtedly encountered the advice that you compile a "to-do list." It's a standard tool of time management. We suggest that you prepare a "to-be list" and a "stop-doing list."

French philosopher Rene Descartes enunciated the principle, "I think, therefore I am." Most people extend that principle to "I do, therefore I am." That's the outside-in approach. We prefer the inside-out approach: "I am, therefore I do." Let who you are dictate what you do.

STAY IN THE BIG PICTURE

Don't lose sight of your big picture as you get caught up in the activity of life. In every problem lies an opportunity, so focus on the opportunity and the solutions. Maintain positive energy. Decide your priorities based on your shared vision, and act accordingly. Just thinking of your goals is not enough; you must take action to fulfill those dreams and make them happen. When your thinking arises from your goals, it results in wise choices that will help you accomplish those goals.

WHERE YOU ARE AND WHERE YOU WANT TO GO

Life balance comes from closing the gap between where you are and where you want to go. To close that gap, you begin with two questions: "What do I want?" and "How am I going to get it?"

Once you have answered those questions, you will be fired up for action. These are relatively simple questions, but they call for deep soul-searching. Your principles and values will guide you to the answers. They will help you tap into the energy that will make it all blend together and happen. Your sense of purpose will ultimately make it clear what your goals are. Your vision will also clarify to you how to reach those goals that you've defined and make the journey more comprehensible for you. Finally, it will erase the doubts and negativity and stop those anxiety-causing questions such as "What good is my life?" or "Why am I doing all this anyway?"

"Everyone has a purpose in life – a unique gift or special talent to give to others," said Deepak Chopra, noted authority on holistic medicine. Note the phrase "to give to others."

Your sense of purpose must involve more than raw numbers. If your purpose is to make $100,000 a week, achieving it is unlikely to give you a warm sense of accomplishment. A sense of purpose must enrich you and give rich meaning to your life.

Nido's sense of purpose is vividly illustrated by his wills.

He has a conventional will that details what happens to his material goods when he dies. That's simply a mechanical instrument, designed to transmit his material assets to his heirs while minimizing the tax burden on them. He lets a lawyer handle that. The ones he spends his own time on are his ethical wills.

He has written a private document to each of his four children that says, "Material things come and go, but let me tell you what I've left for you that will stay with you all your years and, even more important, which you can pass on to many generations thereafter."

This ethical will talks about values, about purpose, about character. This is an example of a far deeper wealth and sense of purpose in life, carrying more meaning than just material wealth.

Finally it is important to know whether you are actually living on your purpose. Self-awareness aids in the making of choices. In his _Journal for Lasting Happiness: Your Key to Success,_ Azim encourages each person to write a daily journal as a habit of self-reflection. When you increase your self-awareness, you understand reality better, and therefore, tend to be more giving. Azim has sometimes found himself doing things that are contrary to his teaching, but his journal writing allows him to catch himself in the act and practice self-correction. Otherwise he would be living an illusion, believing that he practices everything he preaches. Self-awareness comes from asking and answering hard questions that require deep personal integrity.

Living and working on purpose allows you to see beyond present reality to a place where you want to be. You are able to remain focused on your big goals and not let petty things sidetrack you. You feel happy and productive. This leads to a healthy and balanced life. Purpose helps toward Life Balance and is the key to finding your way in the universal puzzle and reaching your destiny.

"The secret to success is consistency of purpose," said Benjamin Disraeli, the 19th-century British prime minister.

As with so many things, Disraeli was right.

SUMMARY:

In summary, you move toward living and working purposefully when you put the following into action:

▣ (1) Articulate what "purposeful living and working" looks like for you.

▣ (2) Prepare your mission statement, responding to the following questions:

▣ What is your passion in life?

▣ What are your unique strengths?

▣ If you had six months to live, what would be most important to you?

▣ What are the different roles you play in your life and what do you expect of yourself in each of these roles?

▣ (3) Seek a clear understanding of the benefits of living a purposeful life

▣ (4) Identify obstacles to living a purposeful life

▣ (5) Work on ways to overcome the obstacles to purposeful living including:

▣ Having a shared vision.

▣ Choosing wisely.

▣ Being willing to take calculated risks.

▣ Eliminating doubt from your life.

▣ Being authentic.

▣ Becoming transformational and not just transactional.

▣ Having intentional congruence.

▣ Focusing on the important, not the urgent.

▧ Focusing on being, not doing.

AN EXAMPLE OF A MISSION STATEMENT:

"My mission is to live with integrity and to make a positive difference in the lives of others; to live a balanced life and to enjoy the process of life. I seek to live to my fullest potential and to be at all times a role model worth emulating for my family, friends, associates, clients, and all who come in contact with me. I endeavor always to be thankful for what I have and to remember that whatever success I have had is through Divine grace."

YOUR GOAL-SETTING EXERCISE

CHAPTER III: PURPOSEFUL LIVING AND WORKING

Which areas in your life require that you work to achieve purposeful living? What is the one big obstacle in the way of your working and living according to your purpose? Set your goal and timeline to overcome this obstacle.

My goal is to work on the following areas in terms of purposeful living and working:

....

....

....

I commit to the following timelines to implement this habit:

....

....

....

GOAL-SETTING EXAMPLE:

I will articulate, in writing, my personal mission statement within the next three months.

> *"Everyone has a purpose in life ... a unique gift or special talent to give to others."*
>
> – Deepak Chopra

DISPLAYING POSITIVE PRIDE, NOT EGO

You can accomplish anything in life, provided that you do not mind who gets the credit.

— Harry S. Truman

QUESTIONS TO PONDER:

▨ Are you driven by positive pride or ego?

▨ Do you take things personally? Do you become defensive and lose objectivity?

▨ Do you often argue about *who* is right rather that *what* is right?

▨ When things go wrong, do you look for people and things to blame?

▨ What is the quality of your personal and professional relationships?

▨ Are you judgmental?

▨ Are you closed-minded?

YOU WERE MEANT FOR SUCCESS

You were brought into this world for success, not failure. Believe it. If you don't believe in yourself, nobody else will. This confidence in your own worthy destiny is what we call "positive pride."

Positive pride is a gift from the universe. We admire the glory of the stars, the warmth of the sun, and the beauty of the changing seasons. These attributes spring from a universal benevolence. We, as humans, also have attributes bestowed on us by a generous universe. With positive pride and self-esteem, we can value these gifts and use them for making a difference. Seeking positive pride means keeping an open mind and dropping the armor we sometimes don to shield us from human diversity. You can't achieve Life Balance by partaking of only one aspect of human heritage and culture. Use your open mind to absorb knowledge from every encounter, every experience, every person, every defeat, every setback, and every opportunity.

You can even learn from your difficulties, tragedies, and enemies. If you constantly learn and grow, you'll discover that instead of being frustrated by differences, you are enriched and enlightened by them. As you learn, you keep growing. And as you keep growing and learning, you embrace balance in your life.

You are a microcosm of the universe. You do not live alone on an island; therefore Life Balance must be cultivated in the midst of others. When you understand this, you make appropriate choices that invite Life Balance. Some people let their egos take over, and they forget about other people or look upon them as burdens or competitors. This attitude creates imbalance and unhappiness in your relationships.

"No tree has branches so foolish as to fight against themselves," goes a Native American saying. We are all branches of the human tree. Let us not fight against ourselves.

In this chapter we discuss the following:

▦ What Ego is.

▦ How to distinguish between positive pride and ego.

▦ Why ego is an obstacle to Life Balance.

▦ Ego vs. love.

▦ Strategies for avoiding ego and thereby inviting balance.

WHAT IS EGO?

"We compete with others only in those situations in which we are afraid and defective in initiative," observed William and Marguerite Beacher.

You can turn EGO into an acronym for Edging Gifts Out. When you're full of ego, you let it edge out gifts such as creativity, innovation, intuition, positive energy, objectiveness, and happiness.

The word "Ego" is from Latin, and it means "the self." To be egotistical is to be self-centered. Far from enhancing a person's stature, egotism diminishes it. As American statesman Benjamin Franklin put it, "A man wrapped up in himself makes a very small bundle."

To the egotist, everything revolves around the self. That's why an egotist often becomes defensive and judgmental, taking things personally. Ego is insidious, because it takes hold of the inner self and eats away at external concerns.

Egotists are not team players; they put themselves ahead of family, colleagues and society. They overlook the immense importance of being interdependent creatures, because they can't see beyond their own immediate interests. They cease to recognize the strength and synergy in diversity, because they are the only entities they're concerned with and their welfare is the only welfare that counts. They cannot be objective, because what they want and what they believe are, by definition, right. They cannot be authentic, because they must buy into the fiction that they're at the center of the universe.

Ego is the latch on a closed mind; it locks the door to lifelong learning. Without lifelong learning and openness, people lose awareness of what reality is and end up making unreal choices. This in turn consumes a lot of energy and leads to frustration.

A closed mind atrophies. So the more open-minded you are, the more you will take from life. When you are open and grateful, you carve blessings in stone and turn your challenges into writings in the sand.

When you are egotistical you pen up your innate talents and darken your light: You edge your gifts out. You also edge out creativity, innovation, love, and wisdom. Ego becomes a stumbling block to purpose, balance, and happiness. It makes you lose your center. It also dissipates your energy. Instead of using it to invite Life Balance, you destroy balance for the satisfaction of your ego.

People with Life Balance see themselves as parts of the ocean and not as individual drops of water. Individual drops soon evaporate or dissipate and are gone. The ocean is permanent. It's hard to let go of our individuality as a drop of water, because we have treasured it for so long. But when we do let go, transformation happens, taking us closer and closer to our essence.

People with big egos are socially difficult, and their self-centered nature makes them hard to co-operate with. Ironically, their "me-first" arrogance seems to rise from a sense of inadequacy and inferiority. Their exaggerated sense of personal superiority is actually a front to mask their deeply felt sense of inferiority. They are really in denial.

Unfortunately, this results in their inability to be objective or open-minded in dealing with life's problems. Therefore, they generally don't succeed in a socially beneficial way. Since they judge success in a very self-centered way, their victories and successes hold meaning only for themselves. They may have intelligence in abundance, but their thinking is distorted. They use a number of justifications, excuses, and rationalizations to make them appear to be always right, without allowing for any other opinion. In their own minds, according to their own logic, they may be right. But they never provide socially useful solutions to life's problems.

People with egos are always watching fearfully over their shoulders, worrying that someone might overtake them. The bird that escapes the ego trap has no fear.

Egocentricity is negative and hampers our lives. As Henry David Thoreau put it, "As long as a man stands in his own way, everything seems to be in his way." It is dangerous when you can't accept criticism, especially when you believe you're wrong. People encumbered by big egos get bogged down with the problems they cause at work with their insensitivity and insecurity.

DISTINGUISHING BETWEEN EGO AND POSITIVE PRIDE

Nido, in his book *How to get Anything you Want,* writes: "Self confidence or positive pride is not bragging about your abilities and accomplishments, putting down the abilities and accomplishments of others, exaggerating your abilities or deeds, out-talking everybody else to get your way. A better word for these practices is arrogance or egotism."

Sometimes there is a fine line between ego and positive pride. You display positive pride when you are confident, open, and selfless. This is healthy and necessary for balance. You have to believe in yourself, because if you don't, no one else will. Positive pride means using this self-esteem to make a difference for others. Egotism means using it for self-gratification and to promote a feeling of self-importance. The balance between ego and positive pride is well explained in this Serbian proverb: "Be humble, for you are made of earth; be noble, for you are made of stars." You have the capacity to rise to the stars, but don't forget that one day you will be buried six feet underground with nothing except what you had when you came into this world.

There is a story among the Sufis about an eagle flying high in the sky, admiring his own beauty, and "looking down" on things on the ground. These egotistical thoughts are abruptly terminated when an arrow strikes the bird and it falls to the ground. The eagle can't believe it has been hit – especially by a piece of metal. Then it sees its feathers on the ground and exclaims, "It is the feathers that made me fly high in the sky and they are the same feathers that make me fall to the ground." The moral of the story is that we all have within us the "feathers" of positive pride that can take us high in the sky and the "feathers of ego" that can destroy us.

People with pride and self-esteem obviously value their own talents and think highly of them, but do not remain centered on them only. They are more open, willing to accept and appreciate, and they are valued much more by society. Their self-esteem places them in high positions, and they can get good results personally too. But their more intense involvement with people around them ensures that they stay socially connected and an integral part of activities, no matter how clever or high their positions.

People with high self-esteem are more likely to reach their highest potential, regardless of what others think. Unlike people with low self-esteem, these people take risks that result in both personal and professional growth.

People with positive pride acknowledge their own uniqueness and can relate to others in a more open and enjoyable way. They realize that they have blind spots and are open to constructive feedback. In this context, compare the personalities of two towering historical figures: Dr. Jonas Salk, who gave away his polio vaccine for the good of mankind, is viewed as a great man. Adolf Hitler, a man who achieved both power and control for a short time, has gone down in history as just an egocentric and selfish person. Both were driven from a sense of self. But while one rose above himself, the other suffered because he was limited by his own ego.

Azim's friend Joe Roberts shared a powerful example with him. He said that if someone is very thirsty in the desert, and you bring a glass of water to share, you have done a worthy deed. But never forget that you were only the "glass." The water came from the Higher Power, as did the air, vegetation, rain, our bodies, and our senses. This is where humility comes in: the realization that it is a privilege, not a right, to make a contribution.

Humility is a reflection of positive pride. It leads to collaboration and synergy instead of competition and jealousy.

Take the example of Dorothy, a dentist who loves her work. She is a selfless team player who focuses on making a difference. When patients come with their toothaches, she spends time with them to empathize and make them feel relaxed and comfortable. She always wears a smile that says, "I am so happy to see you." She is confident, energetic and focused on her mission, which is to make a difference to her staff, to her suppliers, and to every patient who comes to her for treatment. When a patient doesn't appreciate her good will, she reminds herself that the patient's behavior does not reflect her skill or attitude. It is something the patient is going through, and has nothing to do with her. Usually, with her tolerant and loving approach, she is able to win the angry customer's confidence. And even if she doesn't, she does not let that incident affect her for the rest of the day.

Dorothy has positive pride. She does not operate from egotism. She does not edge her gifts out. Instead, she taps into her creativity, innovation, and potential.

Another example is Bob, who is a construction project manager. Bob is a know-it-all. He is a perfectionist who thinks that only he knows what is best for everyone. So every morning, after telling his wife and children how inefficient they are, he goes to work and starts picking on his subordinates and colleagues. He finds fault with everyone, including his customers. Instead of "The customer is always right," his motto is "Bob is always right." He operates

from egotism, and thus does not tap into his genius, creativity, and innovation. He drains not only himself but also others around him.

Self-esteem comes from feeling good about yourself and believing in yourself. It comes from doing your best and leaving the rest, without worrying about others' opinions. It also comes from looking at what is working in your life and being grateful for it.

A pluralistic approach to life is also a reflection of positive pride. It is a universal approach. Everyone – all people and all religions – has access to the truth. The truth is found everywhere.

EGOCENTRICITY AN OBSTACLE TO LIFE BALANCE

As we take a closer look at egocentricity, we learn that:

▣ Egocentricity edges out our innate gifts.

▣ Either introvert or extrovert egos lead to imbalance.

▣ Defensiveness is an energy drainer that leads to imbalance.

▨ Both inferiority complexes and superiority complexes are driven by the ego, and always prove to be energy wasters.

▨ When ego enters, love exits.

GOODBYE EGO, HELLO GIFTS

"It is humility to realize that quality of life is not me. It is us," wrote Stephen Covey and Roger and Rebecca Merrill in their book, _First Things First._

It may take humility to come to that realization, but it is the opposite of humiliating. The person who dispenses with egotism learns that the universe rushes into the vacuum with bountiful gifts for those who care to become a part of it instead of apart from it. When you issue your ego its walking papers, gifts march in to replace it. You become non-judgmental. Your mind becomes more open and receptive to deep learning. You tend to give others the benefit of doubt, which enhances your relationships with them. When ego goes, balance enters.

When you are egocentric, you want constant attention, sympathy, and flattery. You make unreasonable demands. This makes you overly competitive, a sore loser, and a perfectionist. You insist on having things your own way. Self-centered people are not realistic, but are unable to accept criticism and are insensitive to others.

Instead of pooling resources and talents, they insist on going it alone, and though they may be exceptionally good at what they do, they can never match the accomplishments of many able people acting and thinking collectively. In short, they miss out on the value of interdependence.

Azim remembers the humiliation, many years ago, when he was pouring his heart and soul into voluntary work and one of his leaders told him his work was not up to par. Azim was hurt deeply, and it affected him for a long time. He vowed that if ever he became a leader, he would do his utmost never to belittle the hard efforts of others. He knows of people who have given up voluntary work because of similar humiliations.

We learn two things here. First, as a leader, you get best results when you are sensitive to the needs of your team members and try to discover and make use of their talents. Second, if you are part of the team, you are also a leader. Therefore, if you believe in your work you will not let another person's criticism destroy you.

Good leaders see the beauty in their teams. Ego destroys that beauty. Ego in leaders causes them to use humiliation as a destructive tool. Ego in team members causes them to take criticism personally and let it crush their efforts. Azim reasoned that the leader who humiliated him had nothing to do with him. Azim has continued to serve in many capacities, and has enjoyed and benefited from them.

When you don't trust others, you allow them to distrust you. You become focused on the scarcity mentality. A good leader trusts, empowers, and believes in the abundant mentality.

The universe is abundant. It contains 500 trillion stars, by conservative estimate. Our sun is only a medium-sized star; trillions are much larger, and some are very much larger. Our Milky Way galaxy contains about 100 billion stars, and it is only one of about 100 billion galaxies in the universe. So why think in a miserly manner? Scarcity comes from your ego. The larger it makes you feel, the smaller it makes the universe seem in comparison. When you realize the enormous breadth of the universe, you understand how small you are and how much you can benefit from its wealth.

The greatest intellects in history have been humbled by the mysteries of the universe.

"The most beautiful thing we can experience is the mysterious," wrote Albert Einstein, who propounded the theories of relativity. "It is the source of all true art and science."

Jelaluddin Rumi, the great Sufi poet/philosopher, agreed with him 700 years in advance: "Sell your cleverness; purchase bewilderment."

INTROVERTED OR EXTROVERTED, EGO LEADS TO IMBALANCE

Introverts and extroverts are the two opposite sides of the social coin. Introverts draw emotional energy from quiet and solitude; interaction tends to drain them of energy. Extroverts draw energy from interaction with others. They lose energy when they're alone and can't interact.

Neither introvert nor extrovert is immune from the imbalance that springs from ego. An inflated ego makes introverted people sly and jealous, putting others down behind their backs. Egotistical introverts will be quiet and smug, always trying to prove how smart they are. They never accept blame for errors or misfortunes. An oversized ego tends to make extroverts brash, vain, and loud. They love to criticize and to exaggerate their own virtues and the flaws in others. They are show-offs and like to control others.

Egocentric people are ultimately the losers, because they have problems in their personal lives and relationships. Though they can be successful in their careers, they will not be liked as leaders. Egotistical people with both introverted and extroverted tendencies have difficulty balancing their lives, because the negative energy they create erodes their efforts.

An oversized ego will make you insensitive to others, and it will harm your relationships. When egotism is present, love is absent, and without love there is no trust, and trust is the basis for any relationship.

When you block out learning because you think you know it all, it will limit your capacity to be open, to upgrade your knowledge, or to achieve real wisdom. You may possess huge amounts of knowledge, but it has less worth than the wisdom you'll gain by accepting the fact that what you know is dwarfed by what you still don't know and will never master, no matter how long you live.

DEFENSIVENESS DRAINS ENERGY AND LEADS TO IMBALANCE

Defensiveness is an energy drain and leads to imbalance.

Individuals imbued with Life Balance are things of beauty that need not apologize for or defend what they are. They're like flowers blooming in an open field, sharing their beauty with everyone. A flower is not defensive; its beauty speaks for itself. When a flower blooms, it radiates beauty. It throws itself open to the nectar-seeking bee and butterfly, surrendering its sweetness freely and receiving from its beneficiaries the gift of cross-pollenization. Truth, like a flower, puts up no defense because it needs no defense. It gives freely and receives abundantly. A person enjoying Life Balance is leading a life of truth.

Only when egotism disturbs Life Balance does defensiveness enter the picture. Ego-driven people feel the need for armor to protect them from the outside world. They become control-driven as opposed to objective-driven.

Ego often enters on the coattails of superiority complexes or inferiority complexes, both of which are energy wasters.

People with superiority complexes look down on people who are different from them. When this happens, the objects of their scorn may feel neglected, unimportant, and isolated. When they feel this way, you can't rely on their help. You've made no investment in the relationship, so you draw no dividends from it.

People with inferiority complexes think they are incapable of accomplishing the things ordinary people accomplish. That in itself indicates egocentricity. They think their perceived shortcomings make them something special, apart from those who are fortunate enough to possess competence. As a result, they never try to live up to their potential, and all the talent and energy they possess go to waste.

We all are good at some things and not so good at others. Because somebody else is better at a particular thing than you are doesn't make you inferior or the other person superior. Look at the human body. You wouldn't try to tie a knot with your toes, and you wouldn't try to kick a football with your fingers. The Christian apostle Paul compared humanity to the human body and observed: "The eye cannot say to the hand, 'I do not need you'; nor the head to the feet, 'I do not need you.' Quite the contrary, those organs of the body which seem to be more frail than others are indispensable, and those parts of the body which we regard as less honorable are treated with great honor. ... If one suffers, they all suffer together. If one flourishes, they all rejoice together."⁵ ▧

The divine spark that bestows individuality also bonds individuals in a common humanity. We are all from the same source.

The philosopher/poet Rumi put it beautifully: "We are all fellow travelers in a journey of life facing the same seasons of life."

STRATEGIES FOR AVOIDING EGOCENTRICITY

Here are some strategies for avoiding egocentricity:

▧ Be non-judgmental.

▧ Cultivate emotional maturity.

▧ Cultivate objectivity to remain focused and clear about goals.

▧ Invite love into your life.

BEING NON-JUDGMENTAL HELPS WITH LIFE BALANCE

The need to judge others arises from a state of egocentricity. You see the world not as it really is but as the way you define it. You cannot define anyone

---

⁵ ▧ The New English Bible, (New York: Cambridge University Press, 1961-1970) 1 Corinthians 12:21-26.

but yourself, so when you judge others you are really judging yourself. As French novelist Marcel Proust put it: "The real act of discovery is not in finding new lands but in looking at them with new eyes."

When you look for the good in others you encourage more goodness. When you find fault with others, you perpetuate the very behavior you want to eliminate. When you judge, you are continually frustrated, because someone or other does not measure up to your standards. This feeling of frustration makes you uncomfortable to be around. This destroys a lot of energy and leads to imbalance.

As the late author and motivational speaker, Og Mandino, said, "If you have to praise someone shout from the roof; if you have to criticize someone, bite your tongue." And Dale Carnegie validates this point: "You'll find examples of the futility of criticism bristling on a thousand pages of history."

EMOTIONAL MATURITY PROMOTES BALANCE

Childish behavior, such as fighting over small matters and seeking constant attention, shows lack of maturity. It drains your energy in the most negative fashion and brings out the worst in you. Such behavior is ego-driven.

You become emotionally mature when giving becomes easier. You find that it's as easy to give love as it is to receive it, and you don't feel self-conscious or demeaned by it. Maturity enables you to face reality and deal with problems as they arise. With it, you can relate positively to experiences, whether they are good or bad. When you put the needs of others on the same plane as your own needs, you learn to give more freely and willingly. You direct your anger and frustration in more constructive channels than destructive rage. You learn to be relaxed and tension-free, so that your energy can be applied in the best ways possible.

With individual effort and awareness, you can face life with courage and self-confidence. You can face difficulties without letting failure plunge you into despair.

We all move through life at successive levels of maturity. At some point, we put infancy behind and embark upon childhood. The child moves into adolescence, and the adolescent into adulthood. In the words of the apostle Paul to the Christian congregation at Corinth, Greece: "When I was a child, I spoke as a child, I felt as a child, I thought as a child. Now that I have become a man, I have put away the things of a child."

Truly great men and women move beyond the selfish, childish stage as they put childhood behind and enter adulthood. They match their physical maturity with emotional maturity and adopt a more giving, accepting, and compassionate nature.

OBJECTIVITY PROMOTES FOCUS AND CLARITY ABOUT GOALS

"When our self is illuminated with the light of love, then the negative aspect of its separateness with others loses its finality, and then our relationship with others is no longer that of competition and conflict, but of sympathy and co-operation...," wrote Rabindranath Tagore in his foreword to *The Philosophy of the Upanishads*.

To avoid being sidetracked by egotism, it's necessary to focus on the objective and not on your own sense of self-importance. If you are driven by importance of self rather than importance of outcome, you will waste a lot of energy, and that will direct you away from Life Balance.

Keeping an eye on the goal is the key. If you know the goal and have a sense of shared vision, then there is less chance of falling prey to self-importance. Turf wars in the family and in corporations, and, to some extent world wars too, stem from the ego and from losing objectivity.

When you serve, whether at home or in your community, the important thing is the intention behind your action: Is it ego-driven or purpose-driven?

EGO ENTERS, LOVE EXITS

During our many trips overseas, we have found that people, despite their backgrounds, cultures, or faiths, have the same need for love, for respect, for giving and for receiving. This is what makes us all human.

According to the Hindu holy writings known as the Upanishads, "When a blade of grass is cut, the whole universe quivers."

John Donne, the 17th century English poet, expressed a parallel view: "If a clod be washed away by the sea, Europe is the less," and "Any man's death diminishes me, because I am involved in mankind."

Deep thinkers, East and West, understand that the human race is interdependent, and that love is the lubricant that keeps the interdependence functional.

"When the love of power is replaced by the power of love, there will be peace," said Jimi Hendrix, the late rock star.

Love cannot exist in an egocentric atmosphere. When ego disappears, love enters. Love is the greatest gift of all. Love makes beggars out of kings and kings out of beggars. Love can turn an ordinary stone into a ruby; a piece of iron ore into iron. Love is a circle with no end – a sea of unseen shores. Og Mandino, who was Nido's friend and Azim's hero, said: "When you have love, your brows get unwrinkled, you have a twinkle in your eye, your heart opens, there's an echo in your voice, and a smile on your lips."

One day while waiting for his flight, Azim was watching television. A priest was sharing a story about newborn twins, one of whom was deathly ill. The hospital, following its own rules, was keeping the twins in separate incubators. A nurse on the floor repeatedly suggested that the twins be kept together in one incubator and, finally, the doctors agreed. When the twins were brought into contact with each other, the healthy twin immediately put his arms around his sick brother. This instinctive exchange was credited with helping the sick twin to recover. The babies' family and the doctors witnessed the intangible force of love and the incredible power of giving.

Love is a powerful force. When there is love, there is God, and with love your life becomes a work of art, a piece of poetry. With love, an individual is transformed in the same way a caterpillar is changed into a butterfly. It drives home the realization that you have been created and are not the creator. You no longer take things personally or become defensive or suspicious. You can say good bye to complexes – inferior or superior. You'll find no more boundaries and fight no more turf wars. No more Edging Gifts Out! You become a person with an attitude of gratitude. As enlightenment comes, ego goes. Enlightenment thus trumps ego!

REFLECT ON THE FOLLOWING:

▦ Do you take things personally? Why?

▦ Do you become defensive? Why?

▦ Are you working to your optimum? If not why not?

▦ Do you get envious or jealous of others' successes?

▦ Do you let subject disappear in the object?

▦ Do you regularly practice being non-judgmental?

▦ Do you respect all regardless of their economic status?

▦ Do you have love within that melts the hearts of modest people just as the sun's rays melt the ice?

SUMMARY:

In summary, you move toward displaying positive pride and away from ego (Edging Gifts Out) when you do the following:

▦ (1) Display positive pride.

▦ (2) Work on belief in your capacity to achieve your goals.

▦ (3) Realize that you are only using 10% of your incredible potential.

▦ (4) Avoid falling into the egotistical trap.

■ (5) Avoid complexes, defensiveness, and the habit of being judgmental of others.

■ (6) Focus on the objective and not on who gets the credit.

■ (7) Keep an open mind to enhance creativity.

YOUR GOAL-SETTING EXERCISE

CHAPTER IV: EGO: EDGING GIFTS OUT

Which areas in your life require that you work to display positive pride instead of ego?

Ask yourself: "What is the one big obstacle in the way of my working with positive pride instead of egotism? Set your goal and timeline to overcome this obstacle.

My goal is to work on the following areas to eliminate egotism and to enhance my positive pride:

....

....

....

I commit to the following timelines to implement this habit:

....

....

....

GOAL SETTING-EXAMPLE:

I will behave and act as if all my goals have been accomplished. I will create the feeling of victory and success. I will begin this immediately without becoming egotistical.

*As a solid rock is not shaken by the wind, even
so the wise are not ruffled by praise or blame.*
— Buddha

REJUVENATING IN SILENCE

All humanity's problems stem from man's inability to sit quietly in a room alone.

— Blaise Pascal

QUESTIONS TO PONDER:

◈ Did you have fun today? Are you fired up right now?

◈ Do you feel at one with your surroundings at work, at home, in your community, and with nature?

◈ Are you calm and centered when faced with problems? Do you celebrate your joy as well as your sorrow?

◈ Are you going with the flow or against it today?

◈ Are you fully aware of what's happening inside you and around you?

◈ Do you focus all your faculties on the task at hand?

◈ Do you realize you are always at the right place at the right time?

A FRESH BEGINNING

Today is your birthday – your new start in life; a fresh beginning. Yesterday's faults have been released; they are gone. What matters is today.

If your epitaph were based solely on what you did today, what would yours say? As Russell H. Cromwell says, "To be great at all one must be great here now."

Where can you find greatness? Sit still and be silent, and the universe will tell you. When you become silent and still, you tune in to the powerful universal energy. You realize your minuteness and the magnitude of the universe; yet you feel oneness, connected to everything around you. You feel that you are in the zone, and the moment feels like eternity.

This is not idle dreaming. It is not fantasy. The universe is your ally in your quest for greatness. Nature is spontaneous and serendipitous. It is at your service. You connect with nature through silence, and through being in the moment. Thomas Edison said that all thoughts released by all people at all times are picked up and become part of the ether and remain there forever. When you go into silence you can connect with these thoughts.

"Never does nature say one thing and wisdom another," wrote Juvenal, the Roman satirist.

The exquisite beauty of the Universe is priceless. Reflect, preserve and cherish it. Nature is unarguably present. It is peaceful, timeless and awe-inspiring. In it are balance and harmony. It is always becoming, never static. It is balanced and powerful. The mountain stands still and unruffled, despite all the change and noise. The tree bends with the wind. It does not challenge it or fight it. The stars reflect nature's abundance – hundreds of billions of stars.

"Look up into the sky and count the stars, if you can,"[6] ◾ God challenged Abraham. Abraham couldn't count them. Neither can you.

When you are silent and present, you are in harmony with your surroundings and environment. It is very hard to ruffle you; you are not easily frustrated. You pick your battles; you can distinguish between small stuff and the big issues. You pick your company and make appropriate and effective choices that lead to Life Balance.

In today's environment, you seldom have time to immerse yourself in silence. Yet, silence enables you to integrate the many facets of your being. It helps to clear the thoughts and remove the clutter. It allows you to reflect on your purpose in life and on your daily actions. Sanskrit, the classical language of India and Hinduism, gives us the word *Shanti*, which means quietness and silence. It is another word for "peace." Divinity is found in silence, not in noise. When the mind wants to feel important, it tends to invite a lot of noise. Many lessons can be learned from nature: its silence, serenity, and inherent harmony. You feel close to the Creator when you are immersed in silence.

In this chapter we discuss the following:

▨ What it means to be still and present or to "be in the moment."

---

[6]◾ New English Bible (New York: Cambridge University Press, 1961 1970) Genesis 15:5.

■ Why "being in the moment" is an important steppingstone to Life Balance.

■ The specific steps readers can take to live more "in the moment."

WHAT IT MEANS TO BE 'IN THE MOMENT'

"All is contained in the divine breath, like the day in the morning dawn," wrote Muhyiddin Ibn Arabi, mystic, poet, and philosopher of the 12th century.

There is truth in poetry. There is no other time for you except this moment. This breath is priceless. It is your very life. As Mohandas Gandhi said, "We are only custodians of our own breath." The moment now is the breath now. All is contained in the divine breath, just as the day is contained in the morning dawn.

Being in the moment means being quite aware of what is going on right here and now in your own life. Often, your experience does not have this quality of awareness or mindfulness.

When you have your body, mind, and spirit all in harmony and focused on the task at hand, you are most effective and most centered, because you are in tune with your entire being. Balance thus happens in the being, not in the becoming. Ultimately, balance happens in the present.

The destination is in the journey. The process is just as important as the result. If you adhere to a good process, you can expect good results. The process and the principles drive Life Balance and harmony. When you cease to apply principles or pay little attention to process, imbalance creeps in. Concentrate on every step of the activity. Be the very best you can be. Do one thing at a time. When you are able to do your best at each moment, and when you learn to laugh at your mistakes, you experience balance. You remain creative despite your shortcomings. You maintain your high ideals and vision without forsaking your total focus on what is in front of you. You avoid rigidity and remain fluid.

When you are in the present, you find the sacred in the ordinary. You restore your body's need for oxygen and clear your mind from distractions. Grasp each moment with two hands and treasure it. Paint your day with joy and happiness and meet your challenges with enthusiasm and vigor.

"Each minute of this day I grasp with both hands and fondle with love, for its value is beyond price," wrote Og Mandino in *The Greatest Salesman in the World*. "Today is my last day, so it will be my greatest monument of balance."

When you're in the moment, you open up your reservoir of intuitive faculties. Some of the greatest scientific discoveries were made when their discoverers were relaxing in silence, in tune with themselves and nature.

At such moments, as English poet William Blake so beautifully put it, you're able "to see a world in a grain of sand and heaven in a wild flower, hold infinity in the palm of your hand and eternity in an hour."

The insight that led to Sir Isaac Newton's law of gravity came while the scientist was alone in the quiet countryside, where he had gone in 1665 to escape an outbreak of the plague. Newton observed an apple falling from a tree in his orchard and made the connection between the earth's attraction toward the apple and its attraction toward the orbiting moon. From this grew the concept of the universe that guided Albert Einstein and later physicists in their understanding of the universe.

The inner peace translates into outer peace. Spontaneity and poise come when you stay in touch with what is happening around you. Stillness allows you to participate fully in the present. Then your thoughts, words, and actions become aligned, leading to harmony and balance. You are able to think on your feet and make the best decisions. You feel the higher energy levels of the environment and can experience the connections between you and everything else. In that moment of knowing, you see that oneness exists.

By accepting your own decisions, habits, and shortcomings in a given situation, you can be spontaneous, poised, and fully present in that moment. You learn to accept that everything about you is acceptable – that you're good enough for the moment even if it means your spouse is upset, or your boss is firing you. When you are accepting of yourself, these outside events will no longer define you or your self-worth, and you will feel centered and grounded. You will also know what's important right now, and be ready to do it in the most positive frame of mind. This attitude displays confidence, belief in self, integrity, and authenticity. It is the execution in the moment that counts. As Wayne Gretzsy, the Canadian hockey legend put it, "You miss 100% of the shots you don't take."

When you feel closeness with people who are near, they receive your feelings at an intangible level. Azim can remember two vivid examples of this interconnectedness and intangible transfer of energy.

The first arose when Azim and his wife, Farzana, were returning from their voluntary assignment to Pakistan in December 1997. They stopped in Dubai in the United Arab Emirates, where they visited Farzana's friend Farid. At that time, Farid and his family were not affluent by any standard, but they were certainly very giving. They fed Azim and Farzana a hearty meal and showered them with many gifts for their children. Azim was deeply touched by these gestures.

Azim and Farid both decided to keep in touch, but both got busy and made no contact for the next 18 months. It was in March 1999, when Azim was working on his first book, _Seven Steps to Lasting Happiness,_ that Farid came to his mind. While Azim was typing a chapter titled "Experience the Joy of Giving," he thought of Farid, and prayers and good wishes poured spontaneously from his heart. This is what happens when someone touches you with the power of giving.

The thoughts were so overpowering that Azim had to take a break. As he went upstairs to his bedroom, the phone rang and Azim picked up the receiver. The caller asked for Farzana. She's not home, Azim told him, and identified himself as her husband.

"Do you recognize me?" asked the caller.

Azim was silent, not immediately recognizing the voice. After a few seconds he asked, "Are you Farid from Dubai?"

It was indeed. Farid said he was visiting London, and somehow he felt like calling Azim and Farzana.

What we learn here is that Farid gave whole-heartedly to Azim and Farzana, regardless of his financial challenges. He touched their hearts. In return, Azim and Farzana showered gracious thoughts back to him. Second, we learn that when you touch people so deeply, they leave an imprint in your heart, which triggers good wishes and prayers. We also learn that you can give someone energy and good wishes as gifts; so giving is not just tangible things. This energy can travel from one continent to another. Why did Farid decide to call Azim a year and a half after they had met and about the same time when Azim was thinking about him? Some may be tempted to dismiss this as a coincidence. Azim is convinced that it is far more than that.

Another example of vivid interconnectedness arose when Azim was up late one night, working on the same book. He took a break for a few minutes of watching television. Dr. Wayne Dyer, best-selling author of self-help books, was sharing a story about his 12-year-old daughter. He said his daughter loved animals more than anyone else he knew. Whenever he would go for a walk with his daughter, butterflies would come from everywhere, bypassing him and landing on his daughter's shoulders. This would happen every time they went for a walk.

As Azim listened to him, he was struck by the realization that our love for others attracts them to us. The universe is providing signs to you daily. If you remain blind to these signs, you miss cues that you need in your life. Be on the lookout for signs the universe is sending you. By being vigilant and observant, you will understand what really is happening in your life.

When you observe stillness and presence and are open, you will find many such coincidences happening in your life. The interconnectedness will become more apparent. Too much structure and routine can snare you in your comfort zone. Step out of them from time to time and go with the flow, allowing your inner self to guide you.

Silent time means refueling time. It ensures that you are not running on empty. It also provides the opportunity for reflection. It helps you to become present, alert, and focused. Stillness helps with self-awareness and removal of clutter. It invites intuition into your life. People who are in the moment have an aura of peace and serenity about them. They have the ability, in the words of Lao Tzu, father of Taoism, to "be still like a mountain and flow like a great river."

BEING IN THE MOMENT: STEPPINGSTONE TO LIFE BALANCE

The Book of Genesis tells us that God breathed into man's nostrils the breath of life, and man became a living creature. Thus, your life is a gift from God, given to you to hold in trust for a limited time. It consists of a fixed number of breaths. Make the most of the unfolding moment.

Being in the moment invites intuition and inspiration, spontaneity and poise. Don't expect everything to fall in place in a single moment. Stars move in the heavens, tides ebb and flow, seasons pass one after another in their own time. So do all you can in the moment at hand, and if your goal remains unrealized, let go and wait for the season to come.

Don't let a lack of focus sabotage your success. You have hundreds of opportunities to succeed. Some people are so bewildered by the multitude of possibilities that they find it difficult to zero in on just one. They give in to pessimism, and say it's something that can't be done, or they don't have time for it, or the people who succeed are just luckier than they are. Luck has nothing to do with it. Focus does. It's up to you to decide which opportunity best fits your interests, talents, and resources. Once you've picked your target, bring all your resources and talents to bear to hit it dead on. Promise yourself that you'll see it through and make it financially worthwhile.

Applying focus will enable you to brainstorm, research, develop, and refine your idea, and to take it to the marketplace.

You can plan for the next 100 years, but you don't know what will happen in the next hour. You cannot save today's moments for tomorrow's tasks. Time will not be held in reserve. The 86,400 seconds allotted to you today must be spent today or they'll be gone forever. To achieve Life Balance, you have to take one day at a time and treat it as the most important day of your life. Give your whole to the day – to your work, family, health, and spirituality. Greet your loved ones as if it were the last time you would meet them. Planning is good, especially weekly planning, but having done your planning, remember that execution happens in the present.

Often, our lives pass like a stream of cars on a busy freeway. We are conscious of the stream, but unaware of individual cars. We experience events, but they don't register on our conscious minds. The details are not part of our awareness. Like pre-programmed robots, we follow habitual patterns of mundane routines. When we realize how much we've missed, we give way to self-pity, anger, and fear. It can be a real shock to realize just how much of your life is lived in an unconscious mode, heedless of the beauty and wealth captured inside each breath. As Gandhi said, "You are the custodian of your own breath." Make each one count.

It's a lamentable waste to go through life absentminded when, with better concentration, you can be "present-minded." Being present-minded enables you to develop listening skills and to commit to memory what you've just learned or heard. When you're focused on the task at hand, you become much better at resolving conflicts. You become a much better trouble-shooter than someone who comes to the problem with a mind absorbed with other things. You also have more energy to be persistent and to learn more, because you become more tolerant and patient about the situation and its possible difficulties. All this helps you to make wiser and clearer decisions.

Often, when we're not being in the moment, we are absorbed with the past or future. We might be dwelling on some past hurt, or brooding about something that didn't turn out as expected. We may also be spending too much time fantasizing about the future. Yesterday exists only in memory, and tomorrow is only a dream. Today is what counts. Live it.

The need to focus on past grievances arises from a failure to forgive others for past errors. Experienced travelers know that too much luggage is a burden that slows you down, making your movement cumbersome and your trip less enjoyable. When your life is burdened by baggage from the past, your existence can become quite unpleasant. You ditch this excess baggage by forgiving. Forgiving others benefits not only the person you forgive but also yourself.

Feelings of anxiety should have no place in the present. They are always related to fears for the future or regrets over past experiences that could be repeated in the future. When you choose concentration over anxiety or nervousness, you perform better, because all your energies are focused on the tasks at hand. You pay attention to the details and work well, even under the pressure of deadlines.

SPECIFIC STEPS TOWARD LIVING MORE 'IN THE MOMENT'

The following steps can help you be in the present and enjoy stillness:

- Treat each day as most important.
- Focus.
- Concentrate.
- Meditate and reflect.
- Enjoy the Ride.
- Avoid procrastination.

TREAT EACH DAY AS THE MOST IMPORTANT

This approach invites balance daily. Every day is a perfect day. It is the most important day of your life. Plan out what you want to accomplish each day, and pursue it with vigor. You may want to set aside time in the evening to plan the next day's activities. This will give you a head start on the next day. Plan ahead, but live in the present and enjoy the journey. People who have been diagnosed with critical illness realize the value of simple things of life. Why wait for such a situation?

When you find yourself being lazy, look for ways to use the moment more effectively to help reach your goals. Make learning your vocation wherever you are. Have books, thoughts, and ideas ready to keep your mind growing. Memorize pieces of wisdom; they are good for reflecting on in the day and boosting your spirit. Sometimes, though, it's good just to do nothing except to savor the moment.

FOCUS ENABLES YOU TO ACHIEVE BALANCE

When you're focused, you accomplish more in the day with less time and energy. Focusing on the important things and eliminating the unimportant things invites balance. Less becomes more.

Whatever you choose to focus on, study it steadfastly until you become the expert in your field. It could be just one aspect of your field, but it's better to know something inside out than to browse superficially through many different areas.

When you are engrossed and focused, you'll always find more to do and learn. Ultimately, it will allow you to cross-reference and have a much deeper understanding. It is unlikely that such intense learning will be forgotten easily. If things tend to slip from your memory, systematically review what you've learned, and let repetition impress it on your memory. This is how people have memorized the scriptures of Judaism and Islam – by constant repetition. The Sages of the Talmud would repeat any new insight 40 times. They would repeat an especially vital idea 101 times.

You will enhance your ability to focus by first being clear about your vision and mission. Let these be your gauge. Do only those things that enable you to reach your goals and realize your vision. Once you have a clear vision and mission, you will need short-term goals; they will be the steppingstones that take you to your vision. You need to ensure that you have energizing and high goals that will keep you motivated and prevent you from wasting time on unimportant things.

Focus enhances Life Balance. It is the key to turning energy into power. Water tumbling over a waterfall has undeniable energy, but it's only when you direct it through a specific channel that it can turn a dynamo and generate electricity.

Similarly, steam rising from a boiling pot is energy, but it's only when you focus it that it can drive locomotives or turn the wheels of industry. Your efforts in life can be as futile as water over a waterfall or steam from a boiling pot if they're unfocused. Without focus, you'll expend plenty of energy, but very little of it will be converted into real power. To focus steam or falling water so as to harness its power; you have to prepare a channel and direct the energy through that channel. It works exactly that way with life.

Here are eight insights on being focused, taken from an interview with Nido Qubein:

▨ (1) Having a focus is a by-product of purpose. The clearer your purpose in life, the more focused you are on the areas that really have priority in your life.

▨ (2) Good habits are hard to develop but easy to live with. Bad habits are easy to develop, but hard to live with.

▨ (3) Something that is worth doing is worth doing well.

▨ (4) Always give without remembering. Always receive without forgetting.

▨ (5) Extraordinary people always are very good listeners. Make focused listening an intentional habit.

▨ (6) It doesn't matter how much you know or what you can do. What really matters is what other people believe you can do for them.

▨ (7) Our state of being leads to our state of doing. We have to "be" before we can "do." Be authentic.

▨ (8) In business, there are no rose gardens without thorns. Plucking the roses requires fingers that are nimble and tough. Don't let the thorns intimidate you. Consistently execute, stick to it, and persevere.

CONCENTRATION LEADS TO PRODUCTIVITY

The most important things in life are subtle. Yet life, to quote Shakespeare, is full of sound and fury, signifying nothing. The cacophony of the insignificant often drowns out the subtle notes of the important. That's where concentration comes in. If you rush through life listening to only the loudest things, you will not hear the important subtle things. If you tune in to the subtle by experiencing silence, you'll learn valuable things from it. Start by giving full attention to every activity you engage in. When you make the activity the end in itself, you become totally present. When you have this kind of presence, you tend to get involved in activities that are aligned with your vision and mission.

Just being motionless is not what makes you still, but being quiet and allowing silence to take over opens the doors to a deeper connection with yourself. This can't happen if you have thoughts racing through your mind, or if you are agitated about something. Even the most skilled mechanic cannot repair a vehicle in motion. Aren't we all mechanics of our own minds?

When you are silent and completely still in your mind, you're in much better position to figure out what actions you need to take. You can focus on the reality of your situation without getting bogged down in negative emotions. People sometimes call this talking with divinity, and it is true that they receive and understand what they should do with a very clear and simple directive in this quiet time.

"What you are looking for is what is looking," said St. Francis of Assisi.

MEDITATION AND REFLECTION PROMOTE BALANCE

"Meditation is to find out whether there is a field that is not already contaminated by the known," said 20th-century philosopher Jiddu Krishnamurti.

Meditation takes you to realms impossible to understand with the conscious mind. We are so conditioned by our environment that sometimes we forget the essence. Meditation takes us back to the essence.

The best strategy for meditating is to sit silently in an environment close to nature, at a specific time and place, and to be relaxed. Don't try too hard to concentrate; the more you try the harder it will be. Let yourself go like a leaf floating in the river. The leaf lets go and allows the river to take over all control. When you're silent and allow your mind to be still, you also let it rest. Being still does not mean that you are idling away time or not preparing for things. Some people use stillness to make space for God in their lives. In the stillness they can "hear" the inspiration.

Try devoting 15 minutes a day to becoming aware of every aspect of life around you – from the blood coursing through your veins to keep every cell alive, to the insects crawling across the ground under your feet. For those 15 minutes, you are totally attuned to the miracle of being alive. While you're meditating, reflect on the immensity of the universe: The nearest star is trillions of miles away.

When the 15 minutes are up, appreciate how well the time was spent — time that otherwise would have been wasted. Meditation is about concentration. It also helps the mind to exercise control, taking it from a state of complete relaxation, emptied of all thought, to a state of complete awareness of the present moment. Time ticks by with an enhanced sense of consciousness of body and mind. The time you set aside for yourself creates awareness in you. This is true whether you enter a state of meditation or relax in a less structured way.

Of course, the awareness will not come through watching television, making telephone calls, or reading. You can't communicate with your soul while doing these things, even though you're absolutely alone when you do them. But taking time to stroll in the open air, sit with your pet, or putter around in the garden will give you a strong sense of being with yourself. It will allow your soul to talk, ruminate, and stimulate your mind. Be sure to distinguish the worries from more inspiring thoughts, and try to abandon thoughts that weigh you down. There is every chance that you're going to think of childhood friends, revisit places you've been, and converse with yourself about things that you normally would not get a chance to do. It's all good for you.

The power is in the gap between the thoughts – the wider the gap, the greater the power. When you experience this gap, it leads to enthusiasm, intuition, and ease. Your stillness and presence speak. As Li Po, the 9th-century Chinese poet wrote, "We sit together, the mountain and I, until only the mountain remains."

Through quiet time and meditation, you gradually begin to watch the thinker and realize that you are not the thinker. You become at ease with not knowing. Your desire control ceases. You become in tune with the universal energy.

The bulk of the things we worry about never happen. Meditation is the focus on the few things that are important. You learn to listen to the flow, and in so doing you gain insight into the soul. That is a magnificent vista indeed. As 19th-century French author Victor Hugo wrote in "Les Miserables": "There is one spectacle grander than the sea; that is the sky. There is one spectacle grander than the sky: interior of the soul."

Some great basketball coaches make their players meditate. It allows them to relax and learn the art of concentration and focus, which is necessary in the professional arena. Many CEOs of Fortune 500 corporations spend time alone in silence and meditation. This practice invites intuition and inspiration. It also provides relaxation from their very strenuous schedules.

You as a person are much more than what exists in your mind. Identification with the mind takes you farther away from enlightenment. As Buddha said, "The Mind is the greatest obstacle to enlightenment and the end of suffering."

People go to Hawaii to get some silence and a sense of quietness. But they take their laptops and cell phones with them. Every quiet moment will find them on the phone or the laptop, or watching television. What happened to the silent time? Have people become frightened of silence? Do they not see the truth in the ancient proverb that "It is the stillness between the notes that makes the music"?

Azim explains the concept of a balanced mystic in his book, _The Corporate Sufi_. He explains that mystics are those who practice meditation, reflection, and contemplation. Mystics (Sufis) are interested in the essence, not the form. They look at what is inside, not what is outside. We humans have outward appearances – how we look, the clothes we wear, the cars we drive, the houses we live in, and the money we have. To the mystic, these things matter little. It is what is inside people – their character and spirit – that interests the mystic. But "corporate mystics" are people who marry their work with their life missions and balance their work, family, social, and spiritual lives. They are ambitious people who want to do well in the worldly sense of climbing the corporate ladder, raising a family, and achieving material success. But they want to do all this without compromising their ethics and principles. They want to use their success to make a difference. The Corporate Sufi is one who walks the mystic path to spirituality with practical feet.

Let us look at an example of Marsha, who is a senior vice president of a high-tech company. Her very busy schedule makes it a challenge to find time to meditate. To make sure she has time to meditate and exercise, she uses her lunch hour as follows:

▨ 20 minutes to eat a light snack.

▨ 20 minutes to go for a walk in a natural environment close to her work place.

▨ 20 minutes to sit in meditation at the park.

For Marsha, meditation means sitting quietly, sometimes with her eyes closed and sometimes watching the trees, birds, and sky, and reflecting on creation. This allows her regular time near nature and in silence. Marsha demonstrates that no matter how busy you are you can make time for silence if you choose. When Marsha goes home from work, she parks in a silent place for 10 minutes close to her home, gets out of the car, and does some deep breathing and stretching exercises, again while connecting with nature and the silence around her. That 10 minutes, she says, allows her to put her busy day behind her so she is ready to spend loving time with her husband and two young children.

Now, you might say you don't have a silent place near your house. You might wonder what that 10 minutes could do for you, or why you should waste the time that you could be spending with your family or performing necessary

chores. Don't let these thoughts deter you. Remember that there is quality time and quantity time, and that the choices you make either invite Life Balance or repel it.

ENJOY THE RIDE YOU'VE CHOSEN

Do you wake up to an alarm clock or an opportunity clock? Do you say "Good Morning Lord" or "Good Lord it's morning!"? Enjoying the ride starts with having a positive attitude, looking for opportunities within life's challenges.

Every industry has its own culture. Each of these cultures appears to be driven by principles and values. For instance, in the dream-making film world of Hollywood, flattery and praise are copiously showered, but they mean very little. Ultimately, it's the box office that tells you how well a film has done. Compared with the salaries of movie stars, very powerful American politicians are paid relatively little, which shows that power and monetary compensation are not directly related. Power depends on how many people you can influence, directly or indirectly.

Many professionals hardly realize that, apart from their jobs and their skills, they imbibe their industry's value systems. People assume they're safe from influences, but when they ask the question "What will I do?" they need to add another question: "Whom will I become?"

What belief systems are important in your work and industry? Whether it's in pharmaceuticals, medicine, city management, or information technology, the respect and status bestowed on you come only in local currencies and might not be valued elsewhere. That's why it's important that you choose the field that's good for you and the place where you feel validated. It's not only about *becoming* wealthy but also about *being* wealthy, and enjoying the ride toward becoming wealthy.

Make the process of getting to your destination pleasurable and stimulating. We are always rushing through life to get somewhere. The key is to enjoy the ride. We need to learn to be centered despite the chaos. We must learn to enjoy our work and our perspiration. The destination is in the journey. Make getting there all the fun.

Azim takes his young children to school in the mornings. Getting everyone on board in good time is quite a job. So driving to school can be tension time. When Azim first started making the school run, everyone was overactive. Not a good way to start the day. Azim changed his strategy. He drove to school without looking at his watch. He reasoned that if he drove the best he could, nothing could make him get to school any sooner. So he used the time spent on the school trip to have prayer and play games with the children. One such game involved his son, Tawfiq. Tawfiq's challenge was to recite a quotation for each day of the month that had passed. If it was the 15th of the month, Tawfiq had to recite 15 quotations by inspirational personalities.

Playing this game changed the tense atmosphere in the car to one filled with positive energy. In addition, the time was spent in a productive manner. The 9-year-old Tawfiq has memorized at least 50 quotes by great people, ranging from English poet William Blake to Sufi poet Jelaluddin Rumi.

Beauty is all around us. If you don't see beauty, you are not looking for it. Azim regularly drove around Vancouver's beautiful mountains for several years without actually noticing them. Then one day a visitor exclaimed, "What stupendous mountains!" Azim looked at the mountains and for the first time took in their grandeur. The beauty around us is invisible unless we are present.

DON'T PUT OFF THE IMPORTANT THINGS IN LIFE

"Like a candle, we are lighted, flicker for a moment, and then go out," wrote Dr. Napoleon Hill.

A young student at one of Azim's lectures shared a thoughtful poem with the group:

▨ *There was a boy who, each morning, would stack up the letters he'd write, Tomorrow.*

▨ *And thought of the folks he would fill with delight, Tomorrow.*

▨ *It was too bad he was too busy today.*

▨ *The greatest of workers this man would have been, Tomorrow.*

▨ *But the fact is he died and faded from us,*

▨ *And all that he left behind was a mountain of things he intended to do, Tomorrow.*

▨ *Tomorrow was too late for him and maybe too late for us.*

Today well-lived makes yesterday a good dream and tomorrow full of hope and confidence. Do not leave for tomorrow the important things you can do today.

Today is the most important day of your life! Treasure every moment and live your best life just for today.

— Azim Jamal

SUMMARY:

In summary, you move toward rejuvenating in silence when you put the following into action:

▨ (1) Treat today as the most important day of your life. Enjoy the ride to wherever you are going. Enjoy the beauty and wealth of each breath by making the most of the unfolding moment.

▨ (2) Eliminate unnecessary worry – a heavy cloud from the past or the future.

▨ (3) Practice meditation and silence; become attentive and focused.

▨ (4) Follow the motto, "This too shall pass," believing that all major catastrophes are healed with time.

▨ (5) Display spontaneity and presence. Go with the flow. Trust the Universe.

▨ (6) Reflect regularly on the following:

▨ *The value of each moment, each hour, each day.*

▨ *The splendor in a beautiful sunrise.*

▨ *The rhythm of seasons coming and going.*

▨ *The four seasons we are allotted to live (and three are gone).*

▧ *What happens to the path when you arrive.*

▧ *The fact that success is always under construction. (Do you think Bill Gates' success became dormant after he became the richest person on earth?).*

▧ *The fact that the less effort you exert, the stronger and more powerful you become.*

▧ *What would happen if you did nothing for 5 minutes. (Can you manage that?)*

▧ *The dash between the dates on your tombstone – the date of your birth and the date of your death. What are you doing with that dash today?*

"When you die it is not how much you have that counts but how much you gave."

– Azim Jamal

YOUR GOAL-SETTING EXERCISE

CHAPTER V: STILLNESS AND PRESENCE SPEAKS

Which areas in your life need working on if you want to rejuvenate in silence? Ask yourself: What is the one big obstacle getting in the way of my inviting silence and stillness? Set your goal and timeline to overcome this obstacle.

I commit the following timelines to implement this habit

....

....

....

GOAL-SETTING EXAMPLE:

HERE IS AN EXAMPLE OF WHAT YOUR GOAL SETTING EXERCISE COULD LOOK LIKE:

My goal is to invite stillness and presence in my life. I will do this by devoting 10 minutes a day, five days a week, to sitting in complete silence at a park, pond, or lake. I will empty my mind of all thoughts and do nothing at all except to tune in with my surroundings and feel the peace and beauty around me. I will begin this Friday.

From the squalling infant in the cradle who needs everything, the human being, if he lives successfully, gradually matures into an adult who needs virtually nothing.

– Gandhi

PURSUING EXCELLENCE

> The ordinary individual scarcely spends 1% of his time in real production. We have not really tapped human powers.
>
> – Henry Ford

QUESTIONS TO PONDER:

⊠ Do you have an intense interest in your goals at work, at home, and in your community?

⊠ What messages do you give out daily from the way you dream, speak, write, and analyze?

⊠ Are your actions consistent with what you aspire to be?

⊠ Do you realize that it is easier to be excellent than to be mediocre or worse?

⊠ Are you an avid reader, and are you embracing lifelong learning?

⊠ Are you prepared for your next opportunity?

⊠ Do you go the extra mile every time?

You were born with great gifts. You were born to display excellence. When you pursue excellence, you are happier, more peaceful, and at your best; you tap into your potential. Today's challenges are demanding and manifold. To cope with all the demands and challenges and still remain focused and balanced requires excellence. If you are below par, you will succumb to the pressure.

Excellence is not just being good at one thing. You may be an excellent entrepreneur, writer, or scientist and still fall short of overall excellence. True excellence requires that you excel in your work, in your family, in your ethics, in your principles, and in your values. When you achieve this level of excellence, you have achieved Life Balance.

In this chapter we discuss the following:

▓ What excellence is.

▓ Why excellence is important for Life Balance.

▓ Benefits of inviting excellence and Life Balance.

▓ Strategies for achieving excellence and Life Balance.

WHAT IS EXCELLENCE?

Excellence means doing your best at whatever you do. Doing your best requires competence. But that competence doesn't come without effort. As Olympic swimming medalist Mark Spitz put it, "We all love to win, but how many people love to train?"

Excellence calls for discipline and character. It means collaborating with others and inviting Life Balance. Excellence is not competing with others; it is enhancing your own abilities and competing with yourself. It is about becoming passionate and enthusiastic in your work and displaying excellence in the moment of choice.

If you want to achieve excellence, strive to become extraordinary. As Elbert Hubbard, a prolific American editor, publisher, and author, put it: "One machine can do the work of 50 ordinary people, but no machine can do the work of one extraordinary person."

Nido has been involved in his hometown, High Point, North Carolina, where he has chaired campaigns for the United Way, the YMCA, and his church. He has been named Philanthropist of the Year and Citizen of the Year, and received numerous other awards for his accomplishments in business, economics, and education. Nido believes in giving, not as an event but as a pattern. He doesn't just say, "You know what? I'm especially blessed this year, so I'm going to give." He makes giving a way of life. That is the pattern of excellence.

Ordinary people, when confronted with a challenge, ask, "Can I do it?" Extraordinary people, who pursue excellence as a pattern, ask "*How* can I do it." The difference between excellence and mediocrity is the insertion of a single word. That word is available to all of us at every moment.

Life Balance begins within the self, the family, and the hometown. You have to excel in these environments before you can set out to change the whole world.

Excellence is not an act, but a habit. Many of us do things unconsciously most of the time. So once we form the habit of striving for excellence, it becomes second nature, and we pursue excellence unconsciously.

Psychologists say that the easiest way to break a bad habit is to cultivate a good one to replace it. They say it takes about a month for a new habit to become firmly rooted. So brushing your teeth well, eating healthy food, exercising regularly, and reading daily are all habits you can cultivate.

Look after your habits and the habits will do the rest for you.

WHY EXCELLENCE IS IMPORTANT FOR LIFE BALANCE

Excellence helps you achieve balance. The qualities that make an excellent parent, spouse, and worker are all linked. When you form the habit of excellence in one area of your life, you tend to extend that habit to other areas.

Excellence is a good habit. It avoids duplication, repetition, and frustration. It raises your spirit and creates energy and enthusiasm. It creates room, time, and energy to do other important things, thus inviting balance.

Being excellent means being holistic. To be holistic means to look at the whole picture, and not just at its individual parts. When you're holistic, you can't be lopsided. You live a balanced life, with time for your family, service, health, and spirituality.

Leading a balanced life can create synergy and avert burnout. It can allow you to sustain your excellence and continue reaping long-term rewards without compromising your family, health, or spirituality. In fact, if you become holistic, you will start to display excellence in all these areas, because excellence has become a habit.

You are lopsided in your life when you focus too much on one area of your life at the expense of others. Although you may achieve short-term results with this approach, you cannot sustain yourself in the long term. Being lopsided is not being excellent.

Andrew was mediocre in school and in his early working life. After befriending Mark, who was a good man with excellent habits, Andrew gradually worked on changing his ways. He would catch himself doing halfhearted work or stopping short of the extra mile. Sometimes Mark would kindly point out to him where he was falling short. Andrew wanted to make something out of his life. He chose to pursue excellence. The transformation from bad habits to good habits took a long time. However, once he formed the habit of excellence he noticed this attitude trickling down to other areas of his life. He improved his relationships with his wife and children by reading on the subject of how to be a good spouse and parent. He continuously made a choice of excellence in other areas of his life.

The past does not equal the future. It is only a starting point. Make a choice of pursuing excellence and Life Balance. You are the master of your life.

Humans are creatures of habit. When you do one thing well you do all things well. The way you do everything is the way you do anything.

"Good habits are the key to all success," wrote Og Mandino. "Bad habits are the unlocked door to failure."

Life Balance results from preparation. Life will throw opportunities at you – there is no question about that. What is really questionable is whether you'll be ready when opportunity knocks. It doesn't always knock 12 times; sometimes it comes only once. Excellent people are always ready for opportunity, because they know it can strike any time. They anticipate it and are ready for it. They're like Wayne Gretsky, the Canadian hockey great, who was once asked, "How come you're always where the puck is?" He replied, "I don't do that at all. I always go to where the puck is *going* to be."

You need to be proactive to be effective; you need to anticipate things and prepare yourself for them. This leads to excellence and avoidance of failure.

BENEFITS OF INVITING EXCELLENCE AND LIFE BALANCE

Well-balanced people become excellent in all walks of life. They achieve overall balance in their professional, business, family, and overall lives. Their demeanors are unmistakable. You can tell that they mean business and that will always deliver – no matter what. We tend to rely on these people and expect outstanding work from them.

People who strive for excellence are not fearful of change or challenges, but will make things happen despite all odds. Excellent people always do their best and are impeccable about keeping their word. They speak well, look well, and perform well. They feel good about themselves, thus inviting good relationships and Life Balance.

In the corporate world, quality is often described as "free from defects." To us, quality also means providing customers with the products and services they want, the way they want them – with no hassle and no errors. Excellence means that we do all this to an extraordinary degree. So when we speak of quality, we are also speaking of excellence.

An attitude of excellence does not tolerate lax standards. IBM once took a look at itself and found that one operation was processing 96% of its orders perfectly. Many people would consider that high quality, but fixing 4% of the products that were miscoded was actually occupying 58% of the people and hardware. To achieve top quality, we must learn to do things right the first time. Quality must color our outlook on life and our attitudes toward our jobs. Aim for the best and let your customers think of your company as the one that does it right – every time.

Recently, Azim went to a mechanic about an engine problem in his car. The mechanic was immaculate and paid great attention to detail. Azim agreed to let him do the job. Later, he reflected on why he was so impressed with the mechanic. He realized that the mechanic spent 10 extra minutes after he had gotten the job to make sure that Azim understood everything. An extra 10 minutes can make all the difference. It does so at work, and it does so at home with our family members. On first consideration, the extra 10 minutes may appear to have been a waste of time. In reality, it saved a lot of time later on.

MEDIOCRITY AND HALF-HEARTED WORK CAN BE COSTLY

Many people regard a 99% quality standard as quite good, and maybe a little too demanding. How would you feel if you deposited $1000 in the bank and your bank credited you with only $990? That's 99% accuracy. How would you feel if the interest on your home mortgage amounted to $5,000 per year and you were charged $5,050? That's 99% accuracy.

If everyone adhered to a 99% standard, we would be without telephone services for 15 minutes each day. The postal service would lose 1.7 million pieces of first-class mail daily. Doctors and nurses would drop 35,000 newborn babies a year, 200,000 people would get the wrong drug prescriptions, and 2 million people would die of food poisoning.

We would like to put in a word of caution here. We are not talking about absolute perfection. We are just emphasizing that when you become complacent and do half-hearted work it can be very costly. This fact applies in your family as well as your career. If you become complacent within the family and do things half-heartedly it can cause a breakdown in your relationship.

Ordinary people can become extraordinary if they make up their minds to be so. Ordinary people are those who consistently do the things extraordinary people won't do. You can motivate yourself to do the things extraordinary people do, and you can avoid doing the things extraordinary people won't do. The key to extraordinary performance is a willingness to be persistent

EXCELLENCE LEADS TO CONFIDENCE

Excellence gives us the confidence we need to achieve balance. Confidence comes from competence and excellence, not just from positive thinking. It comes from knowledge, skills, and experience. It comes from the people you keep company with, television programs you watch, books you read, and cassettes you listen to.

Confidence leads to commitment; commitment means that you will get the job done without excuses. If education is expensive, ignorance can cost you much more. Invest in education, for it is worth the cost.

"When it comes to the seduction of total commitment, yield," advised Dr. Joyce Brothers, psychologist, author, and television personality.

Some principles for achieving Life Balance and lifelong learning:

▣ Excellence and Life Balance come from lifelong learning.

▣ It is much easier to be balanced and to excel than to be unbalanced and mediocre.

▣ Achieving excellence and balance is a game of inches and going the extra mile. Expand your capacity and achieve excellence.

▣ Excellence means being the best you can be – with passion.

▣ Excellence and Life Balance result from choices.

▣ Seek to learn from your elders and from your role models.

▣ Excellence is a habit.

▣ Excellence is a competency.

THE VALUE OF LIFELONG LEARNING

Lifelong learning is a key to success, because it's about the development of human potential. Lifelong learning encompasses the complete range of human experience. Learning is cumulative. It accelerates; it brings change; it pays. Learning is earning. It civilizes and empowers. It not only teaches but also stimulates. It often is informal. Keeping an open mind and embracing lifelong learning are steppingstones to excellence. So learn from every person and experience. You'll discover that instead of being frustrated over differences, you'll be enriched and enlightened by them. As you learn, you keep on growing. And as you keep on growing and learning, you embrace excellence in your life.

When Nido moved to America at the age of 17, he didn't know much English. He taught himself the language by learning the spelling and meaning of 10 words daily. He wrote them on 3-by-5-inch cards. He learned 10 new words every day and reviewed the 10 from the previous day. He did this five days a week and learned the language in one year. Mastering English is a monumental job. But Nido knew how to cover a mile an inch at a time. He learned the language 10 words a day, five days a week.

By the end of the year, Nido had learned 3,120 words. The typical American has about a 5,000-word vocabulary, so one might say that he was still disadvantaged. But he went on to write several dozen books, more than 100 audiocassette programs, and several hundred videos. They have been translated into 19 languages and sold in more than 70 countries around the world.

If you want to improve your relationship with your children, think how it might work out if you took five minutes a day, five days a week, to do something a little different and non-routine. This would surely excite your children. It's also likely to deepen your relationship with them, since they would have a growing appreciation for their time with you. "Bit by bit" guarantees a good pace for development and ensures tremendous results. Always seek better and more effective ways of doing things. You thereby invite Life Balance.

Our global environment today has the following characteristics:

- ▣ Demand on time.
- ▣ High stress levels.
- ▣ Rapid change.
- ▣ Need to learn and relearn.
- ▣ Technological advancement.
- ▣ Information overload.

THE INFORMATION LADDER

The modern household is awash in data pouring in from publications, radio and television, the Internet and other pipelines undreamed of in earlier generations. But raw data don't lead to Life Balance. They make up only the first rung of a ladder that leads to wisdom. That ladder looks something like this:

Wisdom

Insight

Understanding

Knowledge

Information

Data

Data means raw data, which may be worthless. *Information* is the basic news or facts. *Knowledge* is the application of the information that creates some kind of coherence. *Understanding* is something you have paid the price to master, either through reading, experience, or mentorship. *Insight* is the rare understanding that very few people have acquired. You receive this insight through exceptional clarity, intuition, gift, or blessing. *Wisdom* is acquired through coherent understanding and application of insight. Excellent people gravitate toward insight and wisdom.

If all you have is information, people will use you. If what you have is knowledge, people will need you. If what you can offer is wisdom, people will respect you. Wisdom leads to impact, which is what counts.

Learning encompasses much more than taking in information. It includes the whole area of character, open-mindedness, and universal encompassment. Open-mindedness comes from showing respect toward others and from the humility that acknowledges that you don't know everything. This attitude helps you to invite Life Balance.

IT'S EASIER TO BE BALANCED AND EXCELLENT

Many people look upon balance and excellence as goals obtainable only through arduous effort. Yet, it's easier to be balanced and excellent than it is to be unbalanced and mediocre.

That may be hard to believe, but consider how good you feel about your work and yourself when you are balanced and striving for excellence. Your efforts lead to good feelings within your family and team, and among your clients. In fact, being balanced and striving for excellence can give you many rewards and create a positive energy chain. The reverse is true when you do half-hearted work.

When you begin to enjoy the feeling that emanates from your excellent work, you don't want to go back to your old ways. You realize that the feeling is worth the extra effort you put in. This chain of positive energy is infectious and extends itself in other important areas, thus inviting Life Balance.

EXCELLENCE AND BALANCE IS A GAME OF INCHES

Decide what you want most in life. Determine the steps needed to get you there. Do the first thing to get you started. Every single thing you do a little bit better creates balance and excellence. It's not the one big thing you do well but the hundreds of little things you do better that make the difference. So become an inch better – as a parent, spouse, employer, employee, professional speaker, or friend – and see what a difference that inch makes. Remember, the difference between the person who wins the race and the person who comes in second may be only an inch. When you go the extra inch in your family and work life, you end up with smooth relationships and happy people around you. This leads to balance in your life.

As Nido says "It's not 'slowly but surely'; It's 'slowly and cumulatively.'"

All of us can achieve balance and excellence provided we *want* to improve and are willing to make the right choices and put in the effort. An improvement of a half-percent each day will do the job. If you do that consistently for most of the week, you'll find that your small successes will compound each other and in one year you'll have improved remarkably.

Nido likes to use the illustration of a penny a day compounded. If someone offers you a choice between a penny, to be doubled every day for a month, or $100,000 on the spot, don't hesitate: Take the penny. Doubled every day for 31 days, it will yield $10,737,416. An inch at a time works.

You can apply this principle not only to the career work you do, but also to your relationships, special interests, and domestic chores. If you plan to make positive changes, and if you motivate yourself to perform each task a little better each time, you will have continual success.

This involves the concept that if you do something positive in small chunks of time (a few minutes a day), and you do it consistently – say, five days a week – you'll see improvement. If you want to learn a new language, or improve your relationships, or do better in your job, all it takes is a few minutes at regular intervals. You're doing something special for a few minutes, but you're doing it consistently. And that can do great things for you.

Going the extra mile creates excellence in addition to inviting balance. It may appear that going the extra mile means more effort, and therefore less time for Life Balance. But this is not the case. When you go the extra mile, your work is better and more fulfilling. There is less chance for error and duplication, thus saving time and energy. Imagine going the extra mile with your spouse or child, or with your exercises and spiritual quest. This is bound to help you achieve balance and excellence.

Many people settle for expediency, doing just enough to get by. They don't realize that they are taking a shortcut to failure. Going the extra mile is a long-term approach. It takes effort and often requires that you sacrifice short-term pleasure. But once you go the extra mile, you'll find that the competition is less, and the road becomes clearer.

Going the extra mile means giving more than is required. It also means not only being what you are, but also being all that you can be – in your work and in your relationships with self, family, and community.

As Azim puts it, "People who take the initiative and go the extra mile are still rarities. Emulate them and you will stand apart."

EXPAND YOUR CAPACITY AND ACHIEVE EXCELLENCE

When Azim was appointed the chair of the Social Welfare Board in his community, he had 12 to 15 people in his group. He decided to stage a retreat to work with the group on strategies. He was able to expand his team's capacity by creating several additional proactive teams. This small group of 12 to 15 took on leadership roles in the areas of parenting, and in dealing with issues involving couples, youth, and the elderly. They attracted others to become part of their respective teams. By investing time on education and avoiding duplication by using help that was already available, the board was able to get great results. After four years, the group of 15 had grown to a total of 110 volunteers.

Azim's success with this group demonstrates that extra initiative brings outstanding results. This is true whether one is in business, voluntary service, or within the family. In Azim's case, he had motivated volunteers to help him, and that freed up his time for visioning and moving the agenda of the board forward. It also allowed him time for his family, his health, and his profession.

EXCELLENCE MEANS BEING YOUR BEST – WITH PASSION

When you love your work, you do it with gusto. Generally, this comes about when you align your work with your personal mission. Enthusiasm is contagious; it energizes not only you but also others who come in contact with you.

When Azim was preparing a keynote address for a large real-estate firm, he noted its mission statement:

- ◙ "We are not the best because we are the biggest;
- ◙ We are the biggest because we are the best."

That sums up the results of excellence. When you are good, success and good results follow.

EXCELLENCE AND LIFE BALANCE HAPPEN THROUGH CHOICES

How do you handle yourself when you are tested and challenged? How do you choose your priorities when put to the task? Do you resort to your higher self when faced with the temptation to stoop low? These are choices you make in the moment of integrity, and they can separate the great from the mediocre. The more you exercise wise choices, the easier it is to continue to do so in the future. When you succumb to the lower path, you are less likely to withstand the real tests that are bound to come in life.

Many professionals fall into the entrepreneurial syndrome: They rush to the office and sit down at a desk. Then they start looking for the most pressing thing to do. Usually, they can release the pressure they feel by tackling some simple, routine chores, such as opening the mail or returning telephone calls. Two hours later, they're still caught up in overhead work instead of making calls, generating sales, and earning income. They are caught up in an "activity trap," which impedes the path to excellence.

When you have faith that you can achieve Life Balance, you end up achieving it. Similarly, Excellence means having faith in what you do. This will pave the way to persistence, which leads to improvement. If you keep jumping from one thing to another, you seldom acquire excellence. Excellence requires that you stick to whatever path you have chosen. When you dilly-dally on making decisions, you send the message that you are suffering from a lack of confidence or foresight, both of which are part and parcel of excellence.

People who strive for excellence exude confidence and stand out from the crowd. They are admired for the results they achieve and the spark they create.

Training is good and necessary. But it's education that creates excellence. Animals can be trained but not educated. People can experience both. Education is the ability to think and act from the knowledge received while training. Training focuses on teaching people yesterday's skills. Education focuses on teaching them to develop tomorrow's skills. Education without a vision for a better future amounts only to training.

LEARN FROM YOUR ELDERS

One of the things Nido has always done is to seek friends who are at least 20 or 30 years older than he. He figured he could learn much more from them.

Nido's friends had wisdom, and they were willing to share it with him, thus becoming his heroes, models, and mentors. They gave him information and insight, and had a great impact on him. Some of them would tell him that, much to their present regret, they had invested their entire lives in making money while ignoring their families. Others said they had chosen to make less money while giving their families quality time as well as quantity of time. The irony is that the more the latter group sacrificed business time for family time, the better equipped they became to deal with life's challenges, and the more innovative they proved to be at business. Consequently, they ended up still making significant fortunes.

Azim's maternal grandmother, Fatima, was a source of wisdom for him. A resident of Toronto, she was visiting Azim in Vancouver, British Columbia, around her 90th birthday, so his family decided to throw her a surprise party. It was Azim's job to take his grandmother to the Chinese restaurant where the party was to be held. He learned, via cell phone, that not all the guests had arrived. Azim didn't want her to enter the restaurant until the last guest was there, so he was "stuck" in the car with Grandma for 20 minutes. In those 20 minutes, Azim learned from her things he probably would never have found in books and would never personally experience. She shared with him the story of her arranged marriage, at the age of 14. She told him his grandpa had to go away after the marriage to find work in a different town. She described their move from India to Africa, and the struggle they went through. Azim and his grandmother then discussed whether she would feel safe returning to Toronto by air. She replied: "This journey to Toronto is nothing. The big journey is the one I need to worry about!"

She was referring to the journey back to God. Fatima has turned 97 as this book is written. She still remembers more telephone numbers and birthdays than any of her children or grandchildren. She knows all the hockey scores, and can still crack a joke or two. We cannot underestimate the experience and wisdom of the elderly as they provide us with excellent all-round knowledge. If we're fortunate enough to have them in our families, they can immensely enhance family bonding. Learning from elders equips us to deal with challenges such as the finding of Life Balance.

LEARN FROM ROLE MODELS

Heroes, models, and mentors can help you become excellent. They have already arrived there and can show you the path. In a commencement speech Nido gave recently at a U.S university, he made three important points:

▣ (1) *Who you spend time with is who you become.*

▣ (2) *What you choose is what you get.*

▣ (3) *How you succeed is where you end up.*

To be great you must first walk with great people. If you want to fly with the eagles you have to stop scratching with the turkeys. It's the choices you make, not the circumstances you find yourself in, that define the person you become. The type of success that you pursue in life will determine the kind of destination and legacy you will enjoy.

118

Heroes are people to look up to. Models are people you learn from. Mentors are those who hold your hand while you walk to success, showing you the pitfalls so that you can avoid them. Find heroes who can guide you to Life Balance and success.

Akber Ladha was a mystic whom Azim really admired. He was a very wise man who gave freely of his wisdom and insights. Akber was the one who ignited the spark in Azim to write his two books, *The Corporate Sufi* and *The One-Minute Sufi*. Akber was not alive to see the birth of these books, but he has certainly left a legacy through the inspiration he gave to Azim.

The inspiration we impart to others can go a long way. Shams Tabriz, a wandering mystic of the 13th century, inspired Rumi. Shams wrote no books. Rumi ended up writing 26,000 couplets and became the Shakespeare of the Persian world. Rumi gave Shams credit for all his works.

Is serving always easy? No. There are times when being a volunteer can be difficult. Your family might be upset with you for spending too much time away from home and not shouldering your share of the domestic load. You may end up in a place where people get rude, or do not appreciate your efforts. A volunteer's life is not always rosy. Sometimes things backfire. Having said this, we believe that no matter what price you pay, when you give wholeheartedly and with good intentions, you set power in motion – the ripple effect. And if nothing else, there is an internal instant satisfaction you feel deep within you, which is hard to measure or buy with money or physical possessions. In that regard, it is priceless. So rise above the hindrances that come your way. Of course, we suggest that you always balance your life with your family commitments, or involve your family in your service.

Excellence is not an innate skill. It is an acquired skill that comes from nurturing and mentoring. Your parents, teachers, peers, and mentors, as well as the environment, all play important roles in your achieving this skill. The good news is that it is never too late to achieve excellence, as long as you are committed enough to exercise the discipline and action required. Start today. Take baby steps, and before you know it, you'll be on your way toward excellence.

As Benjamin Franklin urged, "Up Sluggard, and waste not Life; in the grave will be sleeping enough."

EXCELLENCE IS A HABIT

Living with excellence is a habit, and so is living a balanced life. Once good habits are formed, they stay with you. On the other hand, bad habits are easy to develop, but they are hard to live with. Nido, in an interview, shared the following points about good habits:

First, I learned that there are two pains each person suffers from. You either suffer from the pain of discipline or you suffer from the pain of regret. So one of the primary characteristics or traits that a person must have to really develop a solid business is to have discipline. You must be disciplined. You must be tenacious. You must be committed. You must work hard. Most people are willing to work eight hours a day and think that they can succeed that way. You must beat that premise. You have to work hard, smart, and with discipline.

One example is that I read two books every week. Every day I give myself one hour to study on my topic or my areas of interest. By the end of the week, I've read two books. Another example: Every day I write or call at least three of my clients. By writing or calling them, I stay consistently in touch with them – out of sight out of mind. I use another habit. I'm a conflict-free person. I don't want to have problems with relationships. So once a year, the week before Thanksgiving, I make a list of one, two, or more people with whom I've had a conflict or disagreement. I approach them and try to resolve that problem and work through it.

I also learned that who you spend time with is who you become. So if you want to become successful, you hang out with successful people. I learned that by observing heroes, models, and mentors. I learned that by reading hundreds of biographies and autobiographies of accomplished human beings. I learned that by watching the mistakes of others. I learned that by deciphering and analyzing the failures that I have had in my own life and extracting from them ideas and methodology so I can do better next time.

The third one is that learning is a continuum. Every single day before I go to sleep, I have to ask myself this question: What did I learn today that I did not know yesterday? Then, of course, you have to learn that you can be creative, but more important, you have to be innovative. How can we do this differently? How can we do this better? I have probably a million examples of failures. I once invested in a business that I knew very little about. While things were going well, everything was hunky dory. But when things got tough and the economy got messy, I got into an argument with partners and realized that I got into that business based on emotional decisions, not decisions based on reason or logic. Consequently, I didn't know enough to save myself and therefore, I lost a lot of money.

Lastly, I learned that you must have consistent execution. You have to stick to it. You have to persevere. The tipping point doesn't arrive until the cumulative effect takes place, so you do all kinds of little things that eventually add up to the big thing. You can't give up.

EXCELLENCE IS A COMPETENCY

In the same interview, Nido responded to a question about what competencies he had acquired:

Essentially, I position myself as a problem solver, as a solution provider, as an individual who is definitely a critical thinker and can arrive at conclusions that make sense. The way you do that is by having a clear vision about what it is that you're doing. You have a solid strategy about how you want to access whatever it is that you want to access. And, you make sure consistent execution is at the helm."

He also points to listening skills as among the most important you can acquire. In the same interview, he said:

The key always is to listen, because if you have agenda anxiety – if instead of listening you are just thinking up what it is you want to say – you often conclude the wrong things.   .

Listening means I have to hear what you say to me, but more important, I have to hear what you don't say to me. You listen with both your ears and your eyes. You listen with both your brain and your heart. You listen with both your experience and your capacity to project forward. When you listen, you really listen for someone's needs, fears, aspirations, and goals, and then you can bring forth what you know. Listening is a very, very tough competency. Listening can lead to focus. Listening can lead to reason. Listening can lead to education. Listening can lead to solutions. Most people want to fix the blame. A listener will always aim to fix the problem.

Listening really helps Life Balance, because it helps improve relationships and understanding. Being a problem-solver at work, at home, or in the community is a great help and is bound to enhance relationships, especially if tied to active listening.

At the age of 9, Tawfiq Jamal expressed it wisely and precociously: "An ounce of listening is better than a pound of talking."

LIFE BALANCE IN THE CORPORATE SPHERE

If you are a business owner or a corporate decision-maker, excellence demands that you seek Life Balance for you and your team. This means that you must hire the right people and treat them like gold. Your staff should be your biggest asset. Treat it accordingly and you'll have a happy team sustaining productivity. Your staff retention rate will soar.

There are many parallels between corporate balance and individual Life Balance.

In *The Seven Habits of Highly Effective People,* Stephen Covey says that balance and self-renewal are important in organizational as well as individual cases. In an organization, the physical dimension is expressed in economic terms. The mental or psychological dimension deals with the recognition, development, and use of talent. The social and emotional dimension has to do with human relations and how people are treated. The spiritual dimension deals with finding meaning through purpose or contribution and through organizational integrity. When an organization neglects any one or more of these areas it negatively impacts the entire organization. The creative energy that could result in tremendous positive synergy is used instead to fight against the organization and acts as a restraint to growth and productivity. Balanced renewal is optimally synergistic. The same applies to individuals.

In their excellent book, *In search of Excellence* Tom Peters and Robert Waterman Jr. identified eight characteristics of excellent companies:

▨ (1) *They have a bias toward action.*

▨ (2) *They stay close to their customers.* The love of product and customer is palpable.

▨ (3) *They encourage autonomy and entrepreneurship.* They break production down into small components and encourage each to think independently and competitively. They allow for some chaos in return for quick action and regular experimentation.

▨ (4) *They pursue productivity through people.* All employees' best efforts are essential, and they will share in the company's rewards. The language used in talking about employees is different.

▓ (5) *They're hands on, value-driven.* They insist that executives keep in touch with the firm's essential business.

▓ (6) *They stick to their knitting.* They avoid straying into unrelated fields, but remain in the business the company knows best.

▓ (7) *They keep the staff lean and the corporate structure simple.* They operate with few administrative layers and few people at upper layers.

▓ (8) *They're brilliant on the basics.* They combine dedication to central values with tolerance for all employees who accept those values.

When you have such methods in place, you get increased efficiency and effectiveness for your company, your employees, and yourself. This in turn promotes Life Balance for you and your team.

Jim Collins researched a number of companies that made the climb from "good" to "great." The characteristics he identified can be applied to individuals making the same leap.

Collins referred to "Level-Five leaders." These are not headliners or celebrities. In fact, they are self-effacing, quiet, reserved, and even shy. They have a paradoxical blend of personal humility and professional will. They channel their egoistical needs from themselves to the larger goal of building a great company. They look into the mirror to take full responsibility, not outside the window to assign blame.

Balanced individuals have similar qualities. They do not assign blame, but take full responsibility for Life Balance. They also display positive pride, not ego.

Collins also identified "the Hedgehog Concept." Hedgehogs don't begin by creating a new vision and implementing strategies to achieve it. They start their journey by first getting the right people on the bus and the wrong people off the bus. Then they get the right people in the right seats. Then they figure out where they're going to drive the bus. It's a "plan-as-you-go" process that emphasizes that the most important asset is not just "people" but "the right people."

Balanced individuals stick with people who live and display balance. Through mentorship and example they learn to achieve Life Balance. They don't waste time with people who neither display balance nor embark on an effort to acquire it.

Collins identified "a culture of disciplines" and "an ethic of entrepreneurship." By combining the two, you get great results as through some magical alchemy.

All companies have culture. Some have discipline. But few companies have a culture of discipline. Those that have it confront brutal reality, yet maintain unwavering faith that they will prevail. They preserve core values and purpose while they endlessly adapt business strategies and operating principles to a changing world. This combination of core values and forward-looking strategies stimulates progress. The Walt Disney Company, for example, embedded its core values in its mission "to bring a smile to a child's face." Sticking to this core principle helped the corporation prevail over many obstacles.

Balanced individuals look reality in the face through awareness and journaling, and overcome obstacles through enlightened persistence.

Companies that go from good to great have a balanced view of technology, Collins tells us. They never use technology as a primary means of igniting a transformation. Yet, paradoxically, they are the pioneers of carefully selected technologies.

Balanced individuals use technology to help them achieve Life Balance. They don't become obsessed with it.

Companies that undertake change should emulate the flywheel, not the catapult. Aircraft carriers use a catapult powered by compressed steam to give aircraft a sudden boost to flight speed before they reach the end of the flight deck. You wouldn't want to try that with the family sedan. Your family car uses a fly wheel to achieve a momentum that builds gradually with engine revolutions and keeps the vehicle moving smoothly between the engine's power strokes.

When a company successfully executes change, Collins tells us, its executives follow the principle of the flywheel. They implement change not as a sudden, single event but as a steady process. They relentlessly push the giant, heavy flywheel in the direction of change until it has the momentum for a breakthrough. Those who launch radical programs involving wrenching restructuring will almost always fail.

As was explained earlier in this chapter, excellence, not perfection, leads to balance. The companies that Collins saw rising from good to great were not, by and large, in great industries, and some were in terrible industries. Greatness is not a function of circumstances; greatness, it turns out, is largely a matter of conscious choice.

It is the same for individuals: Balance is a matter of choice, not of circumstances.

SUMMARY:

You move toward pursuing excellence when you do the following:

◫ (1) Become a lifelong learner by learning from every experience, every person.

◫ (2) Cultivate the habit of excellence in everything you do.

◫ (3) Go the extra mile every time. Do things an inch better in everything you do.

◫ (4) Become competent in what you do.

◫ (5) Remember that excellence comes easier than mediocrity.

◫ (6) Display excellence in the moment of choice.

◫ (7) Be prepared for the unexpected opportunity.

◫ (8) Obtain not just training but also education.

◫ (9) Learn from others who are good role models.

YOUR GOAL-SETTING EXERCISE

CHAPTER VI: PURSUIT OF EXCELLENCE

What areas in your life do you need to work on in pursuing excellence? Ask yourself what one big obstacle is getting in the way of your working and living in excellence? Set your goal and timeline to overcome the obstacle.

I commit the following timelines to implement this habit

....

....

....

If I follow through with this goal it will make a significant difference in my Life Balance.

> *"In the hands of a talented team, a three-second possession has all the possibilities of an eternity."*
>
> – Pat Riley, NBA Coach

The Winner Within

GOAL-SETTING EXAMPLE:

HERE IS A SAMPLE OF A GOAL-SETTING EXERCISE:

My goal is to achieve excellence in all areas of my life for I know that through excellence I will achieve Life balance.

I will achieve excellent physical fitness by playing squash two evenings a week.

I will meditate regularly to enjoy excellent spiritual health.

I will have a luncheon date with my spouse once a week.

I will invite my children and their family over once a week.

> *The enemy of the best is the good.*
>
> – Stephen Covey

HAVING A SENSE OF CONTRIBUTING

If we are not to live with our fellow men, with whom can we live?

— Confucius

QUESTIONS TO PONDER:

▦ Do you share of yourself freely and unconditionally?

▦ Do you bring out the best from those who work with you?

▦ Are you willing to be the change you want the world to be?

▦ Are you fame-driven or contribution-driven? Do you walk your talk? Do you suit your actions to your word?

▦ Are you motivated to be successful or to be significant?

▦ Do you enjoy relationships of trust and loyalty with your family, associates, and friends?

▦ Are you an active, empathetic and respectful listener?

THE BENEFITS OF GIVING

It is only in the giving that we receive. If you want happiness, give happiness. If you want wealth, give wealth. If you want love, give love. Giving enriches your life with meaning, fulfillment, and happiness. It allows you to unleash your potential and create breakthroughs. In fact, it is a privilege to give. So give of your time, your knowledge, your wisdom, your wealth, your love, and yourself, and experience the power of giving.

In this chapter we discuss the following:

▩ What it means to give and have a sense of contributing.

▩ Why contributing is important to Life Balance.

▩ Strategies for embracing a sense of contributing in your daily life.

GIVE AND HAVE A SENSE OF CONTRIBUTING

You contribute not just by what you do but also by who you are.

"With our words we can only preach," said St. Francis of Assisi. "In the end, it is our actions that teach."

If you have sound character and display honesty, integrity, humility, and discipline, you contribute to others by your own example. Who you are and why and how you do things are just as important as what you do. Thus, by aligning your actions with your words, you become a person of influence and significance.

When you contribute and serve, you tap into your genius and ignite your untapped potential. Most people live and die leaving a huge portion of their potential untapped. This happens because they do not discover their true gifts and therefore never discern their callings in life. They fail to find worthwhile causes that are really meaningful to them and that could make a great difference in their lives.

Each of us is endowed with enormous gifts; most of us only scratch the surface of these gifts during our entire lifetimes. But when we give to others, or give of ourselves to meaningful causes, things change. We expect more of ourselves. We discover new feelings of self-worth. And when this happens, we tap into our potential and benefit not only ourselves, but others as well.

As Azim has observed, "To give is to live; when you stop giving, you stop living."

Some may define success as making a lot of money. Others may see it as building an empire. Some define it as beating a baseball record, and some as unraveling the secrets of the universe. Still others define it as feeding the hungry children. How do you define success?

The happiest people are those who focus on purpose and giving. You must travel the journey from success to significance. This happens when you begin to give and make a difference.

During Expo 1986 in Vancouver, British Columbia, Azim decided to take Gale, a wheelchair-bound friend, to visit the Expo. He picked her up at her house, patiently seated her in his car, put the wheelchair in the trunk, and proceeded to Expo.

When they reached Expo, they encountered a huge crowd with long lines everywhere. Azim felt that he had goofed badly by not thinking things through. He wondered how they would ever be able to wade through the crowd and negotiate the lines to see the shows. But since they had come all this way, Azim decided that they should take in at least a few shows. So they both waited in line.

After a few minutes, a police officer passed by and saw Gale in the wheelchair. He asked Azim and Gale to follow him. He took them to the front of the line, and told them that they could do the same thing at the rest of the shows. They saw most of the shows in a fraction of the time it would have taken Azim to see the Expo on his own. He was rewarded for his kind gesture.

It doesn't always work out that way. But had the officer not appeared, Azim would still have persevered to ensure that Gale was able to experience the Expo. It's the intention that counts.

If you're like most people, you've been through difficult times with a friend who has a serious illness, or is hurting from a divorce, or is coping with some other difficult event in life. You have to balance the compassion, time, and energy you offer to such friends with your own ability to give. You have to be cautious not only for your own personal interest but also for theirs, because you want to empower, not overpower.

Rebecca approached Azim and shared her dilemma: "My husband is unreasonable; he does not care about me. My mother-in-law is the boss, and whatever she says my husband follows. I really feel wasted and am not using my creativity and genius. I am doing menial work, and my life is totally unbalanced."

She told him of many things that were amiss in her life. Azim noticed that all her complaints were about other people. She was allowing them to control the way she felt. As long as this continued, she would continue to have problems until other people changed. That made it a totally helpless situation.

Azim discussed with Rebecca ways that this situation could change. It was soon apparent to Rebecca that if she wanted to effect change it would have to begin with herself. She had to take 100% responsibility for creating change. It was her choice. She decided to become the change agent – a person with a sense of contributing. This is how she did it:

With her husband: She engaged her husband in a discussion of his ideals, goals, and visions. She was amazed at how similar his goals were to her own. By understanding his ideals, she was able not only to influence and contribute to them but also to invite his interest in *her* ideals and goals.

With her mother- in- law: She began by asking her about her childhood dreams, inspirations, and experiences. She was really taken aback by the struggles and challenges her mother-in-law had gone through. She began to reflect more deeply upon her relationship with her mother-in-law. This reflection was a major challenge for her. Rebecca began to understand why her mother-in-law behaved the way she did. It did not justify her behavior, but knowing what lay behind the behavior helped Rebecca understand her better. This dialogue made Rebecca see her mother-in-law in a different light, and it enabled her to appreciate her better. It also made the mother-in-law feel important and valued; she realized that no one in the last few years had asked her about her childhood. This, of course, enhanced Rebecca's standing in her eyes.

WHY CONTRIBUTING IS IMPORTANT TO LIFE BALANCE

Life Balance comes from feeling worthy of yourself. This self-worth comes through the contributions you make. The benefits of giving run both ways. The more you help others, the more you help yourself. The more you give, the more you have, the more you find, and the more you receive.

"Give when the season of giving is here so that your coffer is not empty when you die," wrote Kahlil Gibran. Giving is an effective way of filling your spiritual coffers.

Having a sense of giving brings meaning and fulfillment. It creates positive energy, allowing you not only to handle other challenges but also to move proactively toward Life Balance. You come home from work satisfied, having made a difference. You're eager to go back to work the next day. It's a great feeling.

Contributing creates significance, value, happiness, and balance. When you are making a contribution you feel valuable. People want to be around you. You have better relationships at home and at work, and you are more energetic. You waste less time and energy on things that matter least. You tap into your creativity and potential because you do things for the right reasons. Having a sense of giving makes you feel and act worthy. You thus end up doing worthwhile things at work, in your family, in your community, and in society. You tap into genius by working on your calling and giving to worthwhile causes, thereby cultivating excellent habits. You experience the power of giving.

Some professional careers, by their very natures, allow you to make contributions to society. Physicians, teachers, and nurses benefit humanity directly just by doing their jobs. But you can make a difference to others while pursuing any career. Every career offers opportunities to show genuine concern and compassion toward those you come in contact with. Every career allows you to earn a living without taking advantage of others.

As the Dalai Lama put it: "If in day-to-day life you lead a good life, with honesty, with love, with compassion, with less selfishness ..., automatically it will lead to Nirvana." And to the Buddhist, Nirvana is bliss.

Japan's economic growth following World War II was a major 20th-century success story. The growth was not based on competition. Its fundamental element is expressed in the Japanese word *kyosei*, which means a spirit of cooperation. When you follow a sense of contributing, you think in terms of cooperation, not competition. All great leaders are givers who contribute not only to their own richness but also to that of the people they lead. If you apply this philosophy of *kyosei* in your life, it will help you attain Life Balance.

In the state of Gujarat in northwestern India, the Aga Khan Rural Support Program provides a vivid example of the spirit of co-operation. Farmers in each village are taught to combine their efforts and strengths for the common good of the village. They have collectively created waterways and provided irrigation for their respective villages. With a little foresight and sacrifice, these poor farmers have now created a better future for themselves.

Azim sums up the principle of giving and receiving in this passage from his book, *The Corporate Sufi*:

Keep the flow going. A river stagnates if it stops flowing, a cow does not receive more milk if it stops giving milk, and a sheep does not receive more wool if it does not share its wool. When the flow stops, receiving stops. Ask yourself: Are you in the flow? Do you live as a conduit receiving with one hand from your Creator and giving with another, thus increasing the flow through you?

STRATEGIES FOR CONTRIBUTING IN OUR DAILY LIVES

In this section we cover the following areas:

- Contributing through small acts of consideration.
- A win-win for giver and receiver.
- Striving for significance, not just success.
- Striving to enjoy meaningful relationships.
- The requirement of small sacrifices in giving.
- Giving to charitable institutions and community.
- Servant – leadership.
- Becoming influential to others.
- Welcoming guests at home.
- Giving extraordinary service.

CONTRIBUTION THROUGH SMALL ACTS OF CONSIDERATION

Once, when Azim and his family were driving in Los Angeles, they saw what seemed to be a dead bird lying in the road. Azim drove past it and almost ignored it. Then something compelled him to drive around the block and return to the bird. He got out and placed the bird on the side of the curb. To his utter surprise, the bird trembled and stirred, and as they drove away, it flew into the air. Apparently it had been lying on the main road injured and needed a little support to get back on its wings. Had Azim left the bird, another motorist might have crushed it. How little effort it sometimes takes to save a life! And it set an excellent example for Azim's children, who were in the car.

Small acts of kindness make a difference. The difference may not be anything big; in fact, many relationship issues arise because of small things. But if you begin giving in small ways, whether at home, at work, in your community, or in the natural environment, you build momentum toward becoming a holistic person with a sense of giving.

At the end of Nido's sophomore year at Mount Olive College, he had saved $375 to buy a car. The cheapest one he could find cost $750. He was disappointed but not discouraged. He knew that if he saved more money he could eventually buy a car. He related the story to Verta Lawhon, his housemother. She had little financial means. She was just a great listener. She made $100 a month from Social Security and received $100 a month more from the college for serving as mother-in-residence. At the end of that month, Nido received a bank statement reflecting a balance of

$750, even though he knew it should have been only $375.

He told Miss Lawhon about it, thinking that perhaps the bank had added incorrectly. Or had it? Could it be that this woman, making only $200 a month, had contributed $400 to a struggling student to buy a car?

She had indeed. She explained: "I've decided it's much better for me to invest my money in the life of a budding young man than to park it in my savings account."

That was a huge turning point for Nido. It taught him that it is always better to give than to receive. As William Barclay, the Scottish theologian, says, "Always give without remembering, and always receive without forgetting." Miss (Ms.?) Lawhon taught Nido about sacrifice and generosity. From that point on, he lived by the principle Azim enunciated: "The more you are in the flow of abundance, the more abundance flows through you."

THE GIVER BENEFITS AT LEAST AS MUCH AS THE RECEIVER

Azim, after moving from England to Canada in 1980, began giving rides to elderly and sick people who couldn't get around. He took them to church and ran errands for them. He found himself using a lot of gasoline in his big white Canadian Pontiac. Since he had just moved and was sleeping on the couch at his friend's house, he didn't have much money. At one point, he wondered whether he could continue giving rides.

Then his boss, Harold Karro – a kind man who later became his partner – gave him two gasoline credit cards as a business perk. The gift enabled Azim to continue rendering kindness to the sick and elderly. Azim believes his boss's generosity was triggered by the good wishes and prayers of the people who befriended him. To this day, they are Azim's fans, and they greet him whenever they see him from a distance.

"It is one of the beautiful compensations of this life that no one can sincerely try to help another without helping himself," wrote Ralph Waldo Emerson, the 19th-century American philosopher-poet.

FROM SUCCESS TO SIGNIFICANCE

In an interview with John David Mann for the magazine *Networking Times*, Nido was asked about the difference between success and significance. Nido responded as follows:

We talk about "success" as if it were the end result of life's best journey, but that's not so. I meet people all the time who make a million dollars a year and ask, "If I'm so darned successful, why am I so miserable?" If your life is merely successful, but devoid of significance, you simply cannot experience the fullness of life.

Success is secular by any measure; significance is spiritual by every measure.

Success talks about creativity; creativity asks the question, "How can we do this differently?" Significance talks about innovation; innovation asks the question, "How can we do this better?"

Success talks about the three Fs of achievement: If you have your fans, your fame and your fortune, you've really done something. What a sad way to measure one's life accomplishments!

Significance talks about the three Fs of appreciation: faith, family, and friends. If you have a sufficient supply of faith, family and friends, you'll live life deeper, wider, and at a higher level than most people ever discover.

We need to be mindful of our actions on a daily basis. We need to ensure that we are making a significant difference to those around us and that we are adding life to our years and not years to our life. We would like to add that one act of kindness could be the catalyst that triggers a whole chain of similar acts.

When Nido was a student at Mount Olive College, he worked 10 hours every day just to be able to go to school. He finished his sophomore year and was getting ready to transfer to High Point University – the institution he now heads. The president of Mount Olive College approached Nido with the news that, even though he had worked 10 hours a day, it hadn't been enough to pay all his school expenses. In fact, there was big gap between the money he owed the school and the money he had already paid. But an anonymous ~~doctor~~ physician in a neighboring city had picked up the difference and paid it to the school on Nido's behalf. Nido was so touched by the doctor's generosity, he wanted to meet and personally thank him for his extraordinary kindness. But the doctor wished to remain anonymous. So Nido went to his dormitory room, knelt beside his bed, and made a commitment to God that when he began to earn money, he too, in some way, would initiate a fund to help students go to college.

That was the birth of an idea. Nido acted on it when he began his business in 1973. In the first year, he was able to give only one scholarship, worth $500. Today, Nido's foundation gives out about 50 scholarships annually, totaling about $200,000. Altogether, his foundation has awarded about $3 million to 600 deserving students. Try to visualize the snowballing effect of these 600 students turning around and committing similar acts of significance. An incredible story!

When people ask Nido what areas of his life give him great joy, he always cites the Qubein Foundation as a source of great satisfaction and significance for him.

Nido proves the validity of the principle: "Sow sparingly, reap sparingly; sow bountifully, reap bountifully."

The interviewer for _Networking Times_ asked Nido how success and significance relate differently to giving. Nido responded:

Significance makes a clear distinction about giving back. You often hear successful people say, "This community has been good to me, my alma mater's been good to me, I must give back."

God is not pleased with people who simply give back. People who view their stewardship in a role of giving back miss the point. Significance focuses on giving, period. Not giving back. Not giving as payment. It's the same as with loving; as a parent, you don't love your child because the child loves you first. You don't "love back" to your child. You love your child – period – even when that child is perhaps unlovable. ...

Giving isn't about the fact that you're my friend and you've asked me to give; giving is about sharing from your heart. It's not that giving back is in itself a bad thing, but it's when you graduate from giving back to giving that you arrive at the zenith of true pleasure.

William Barclay, the Scottish theologian, said something wonderful about giving: "Always give without remembering. Always receive without forgetting." That has been a mantra for me.

There are many ways one can give without any financial resources: You can give talent, skill, time, love, caring, ingenuity; you can mentor someone, coach someone, advise, guide, or serve as a role model. These are all avenues of giving.

There are four kinds of capital. Financial capital everyone understands. There is also educational capital, which is what Networking Times shares with its readers. Then there's reputational capital; when you have a good reputation, people are willing to listen to you and do business with you.

Finally, you have relational capital – perhaps the most important of all. What truly makes you rich is the depth of all your relationships. My friend Robin Sharma wrote a book called, Who Will Cry When You Die? That kind of puts things in perspective.

STRIVE TO ENJOY MEANINGFUL RELATIONSHIPS

Once Azim went to the airport to pick up someone who had come to attend a funeral. While waiting, he met a woman from his community, and they began talking about death. The woman shared something very powerful. She told Azim that when she was young she had a sister but no brother. The parents

143

wanted to have a son, but for years seemed unable to have another child. At last, a son was born to them.

In time, the woman went to England to study. She had little contact with the brother, except during short vacation visits.

Then the brother became critically ill. The sister flew home from England and stayed constantly at her brother's side for the final six weeks of his life. She told Azim that during those six weeks she bonded with him, and they became the best six weeks of her life. She said that even though she missed her brother intensely, the memories of those six weeks were so powerful that she would be forever grateful for the experience. She said that if God had given her a choice between having her brother for the short time he lived or not having him at all, she would have picked the former. Those six weeks of bonding by his bedside were equivalent to a lifetime, she said.

Azim told this story to a group of cancer patients, one of whom shared a similar story about three weeks spent at the bedside of her dying mother.

She said she bonded more with her mother during those three weeks than she had done in a lifetime.

Eventually, we all leave this life empty-handed. After you die, it will not matter how big your house or bank account was. But the world can be a better place because, while you were here, you gave of yourself. This concept really hit home. How is it that the few weeks in the lives of those two women produced bonding more powerful than people sometimes encounter during 60 years of togetherness? Many people who have been married for decades could never relate to those experiences. We believe these magical experiences happen because powerful giving and receiving are going on at a very deep level.

The amount of time spent with family is important, because quantity sometimes results in quality. But ultimately, the biggest difference results from undivided quality time spent with those dear to you.

Love is a powerful force that creates giving and significance. For Mother Teresa, seeing a sick person die with a smile on his face rather than in agony and misery made her work significant.

GIVING MAY REQUIRE SMALL SACRIFICES

Sometimes, giving up something brings as much joy as giving away something. The principle is illustrated in the story about a king who was giving away gold coins to the people of his kingdom.

As his subjects lined up to receive their coins, the king noticed a saint who had lined up with them. Every time it was his turn to get the coin, he let the person behind him go ahead. Then he returned to the end of the line. The king finally asked him to explain what he was doing.

"I have no gold coins," replied the saint, "but I want to share in the giving. So I'm giving up my turn."

WELCOMING GUESTS AT HOME

Visitors bring abundance to your house, even though they may also bring some discomfort and inconvenience.

Some guests bring wisdom for your children and new friendships for the family. And when you are generous with your hospitality, you teach your children to give.

Of course, you'll encounter the odd person who takes advantage of your generosity. When that happens, you'll still be ahead if you allow the ingrate to tap into your reserve capacity, as long as it does not ruin your relationship with your family.

Shaffin and Azmina are Azim's brother and sister-in-law. They live in Dar es Salaam, Tanzania, Azim's birthplace. In the past few years, Shaffin and Azmina have received many relatives and friends as guests. Each one has been highly complimentary of their hospitality and generosity. It is no wonder that they are blessed with abundance and happiness. Their young children have learned to be equally giving and loving.

GENEROSITY ON THE STREET

"In every seed," wrote Deepak Chopra, "is the promise of thousands of forests, but the seed must not be hoarded; it must give its intelligence to the fertile ground. If you give grudgingly, there is no energy behind that giving."

It's easy to be generous with friends and family — people we know, love, and trust. Generosity comes a little harder when the object is a stranger whose values and habits we don't know; when the only thing we know for sure is that the person is in dire straits for one reason or another. Azim's friend Alykhan encountered one such person, a panhandler on the streets of Vancouver. Here's Alykhan's story:

One night, I happened to be out with some friends on my way to a nightclub somewhere in downtown

Vancouver. As I was waiting to cross the street, a man approached me. He asked me if I could spare some change. He said that he had AIDS and only six months to live. He had lost his job and had no food or money. I asked him what he would do with the money if I gave it to him. He said he would buy food. This was an area of Vancouver in which people were known to buy drugs, and I was concerned that he would use the money to buy himself a "fix." We happened to be standing outside a convenience store. So I said to him, "Let's go shopping."

We went inside and I told him to pick out everything he needed. He picked up milk, boxes of cereal, bags of chips, some soft drinks and other incidentals. The total bill came to less than $20. He was the happiest man on Earth. To me, it seemed only natural to help this person. Most people ignore the panhandlers and beggars on the streets of Vancouver.

GIVING TO CHARITABLE INSTITUTIONS AND COMMUNITY

Donating to charitable institutions is a great way to make a difference. This type of generosity feeds hungry children, looks after orphans, and gives our communities a feeling of being protected and looked after. It helps artists, institutions, and those who need a bit of a boost to get started. Charitable organizations provide their own rewards for people who contribute. The givers come away with a sense of having contributed to a worthy cause. Money from charities sometimes sustains entire families. And charitable giving may be rewarded with tax breaks for companies and individuals.

An average Silicon Valley family contributes about $2,300 to non-profit organizations each year, and this money obviously is enough to sustain many worthy causes. It also helps employees to claim maximum tax deductions. It keeps estate taxes down and helps donors to avoid capital-gains taxes. These days, non-profits also accept stock donations, and some have started taking real-estate gifts too.

Azim has been an active member of his community for a long time. His speaking skills were honed within the community, and so were his voluntary and leadership skills. Azim's father and grandfather were both volunteers for many decades. Azim's daughter, Sahar, age 15, and son, Tawfiq, age 9, are both volunteers in the community, and both are learning leadership skills at an early age. The win-win factor is that all of them are learning leadership skills, are bonding, and are involved with the community. Their common service provides an opportunity for family bonding while contributing to the well-being of the community. All of this promotes Life Balance.

SERVANT LEADERSHIP

Servant leadership is about being a resource, not a crutch, to your team. Servant leaders put themselves at the disposal of the team instead of making themselves the masters of team members. They are there when needed and they get out of the way when they aren't.

Servant leadership is about empowering others. It allows the leader to offload some responsibilities from his shoulders, thus allowing time for him to bring balance to his own life. If you are too much the control freak, balance becomes harder. The irony is that the more you let go of control, the more in control you become.

This type of leadership also recognizes the need to praise good behavior and applaud good results. The more you catch people doing things right, the more right things they do. This creates effective results, thus giving more space to you for other areas of your life.

One of the best gifts we can give our children is to inspire them to be givers. Both Nido and Azim were blessed with parents who exemplified the beauty and joy of giving. So they not only learned from what they were told, but they also watched giving in action. Because of their experiences with their own parents, giving comes naturally to both of them, and they are eternally grateful for it.

"A rich life," writes philosopher and theologian Cornel West, "is fundamentally a life of serving others, a life of trying to leave the world a little better than you found it."

Every one of us can have a rich life if we choose. A first step is simply to become a more giving person.

BECOMING INFLUENTIAL TOWARD OTHERS

In an interview with business coach and consultant Simon Vetter, Nido was asked who was the biggest influence in his life. He responded:

The single most influential person in my life was my mother, who had a fourth grade education. But I'd put her against 25 Ph.D.s from the finest Ivy League schools of your own picking. This woman worked day and night to feed five of us in the family because my father had died when I was six years of age. She went on to instill in our hearts and minds solid wisdom and very fruitful, purposeful, and meaningful suggestions, recommendations, and guidelines for living life to the fullest.

My mom would say, for example, "Always learn from the experts because the experts have their knowledge in order." If your knowledge is not in order, then the more of it you have, the more confused you become. Meaningful change comes from within, so make sure you change yourself from the inside out. When you do that, you will find that while every improvement is the result of change, every change does not necessarily result in improvement.

My mother was a very large influence in my life. Later, I had many other influential people – business people and industrialists whose names may not be known to everyone, but they are community leaders from whom I have learned all kinds of things. One of these is William Horney. He's now about 84-85 years young. He's a man who built a business, an industrial leader, a highly respected community leader, and an individual who understands that it's better to give than to receive. He understands the basic principals of how to run a business, how to be a transformational leader. I met him when I came to High Point, North Carolina, through a social gathering. We became friends and one thing led to another. Eventually, he became the chairman of the Board of Trustees for my scholarship foundation, and obviously, we became very close. We met frequently and we talked often. Formally and informally, we interacted and dialogued about life. Through osmosis, observation, advice, and guidance, he molded much of my thinking and contributed much to my ability to be a leader myself.

EXTRAORDINARY SERVICE IN A CORPORATE ENVIRONMENT

Giving extraordinary service is one way of achieving Life Balance. The greater your service to others, the higher your rewards will be. If you want to increase your rewards in life, increase your service. Do ordinary things in extraordinary ways, and see how your rewards increase. We recommend that you serve unconditionally – without any expectation. You will be rewarded for your service, either tangibly or intangibly.

When you serve at work, you also begin serving at home. It becomes a habit. The way you do anything is the way you do everything. Managers who motivate have very definite results in mind; they use an employee's talents more than they depend on their own skills or experience, and they get the appreciation of the staff at the same time.

Success can happen at work only when people have a deep sense of purpose in their lives, and when they feel that they make a difference. A worker's personal reasons for being at a job and the purpose of the job itself should be in alignment. The worker should feel part of something bigger than the task of the moment. When people get the opportunity to learn and develop, get recognition for their contributions, and work in a friendly atmosphere, chances are that they'll be happier for a longer time than they would be at a place where they're paid well but receive little else. A supervisor's attitude toward the staff has a tremendous effect on the staff's attitude toward its place in the corporation.

When managers are able to keep communication open and to keep it honest, they help employees develop their skills and enable them to keep the learning process open. They make them aware of the bigger picture involved in their contribution to work. In this way, they can earn the loyalty of their employees and be able to retain their services longer.

Money has its own place, and it is irreplaceable for those who are looking for ways to meet their basic needs. But other commodities have values that can't be expressed in monetary terms. You can give others your honesty, and that gift can never make you poor. You can get rich by lying, but the lies won't bring you happiness.

Give others your respect, your care, and your compassion: This world needs nothing more than it needs compassionate people who care and are concerned about others. Give others your energy as well, and let them be fired up with a sense of excitement toward life. Give them your experience, so that they can learn from your efforts and mistakes.

"Service is the rent we pay for being," said Marian Wright Edelman, founder of the Children's Defense Fund. "It is the very purpose of life, and not something you do in your spare time."

And the better the space you occupy, the higher the rent. Let us all emulate the attitude of the Dalai Lama: "As long as space remains, so long as sentient beings' suffering remains, I will remain, in order to help, in order to serve..."

SUMMARY:

In summary, you move toward having a sense of contributing when you do the following:

⊠ Share of yourself freely and unconditionally.

⊠ Go from success to significance.

⊠ Be contribution-driven, not fame-driven.

⊠ Give at work and at home, and make giving a habit.

⊠ Give extraordinary service and become a leader.

⊠ Give tangible gifts such as money and things, as well as intangible gifts such as honesty, love, and respect.

⊠ Strive for *kyosei* — cooperation, not competition.

YOUR GOAL-SETTING EXERCISE

CHAPTER VII: SENSE OF CONTRIBUTING

What areas in your life do you need to work on to have a sense of contributing? Ask yourself: "What one big obstacle is getting in the way of my achieving a sense of contributing?" Set your goal and timeline to overcome this obstacle.

My goal is to work on the following areas in terms of my sense of contributing:

....

....

....

I commit to the following timelines to implement this habit

153

....

....

....

If I follow through with this goal it will make a significant difference in my Life Balance.

GOAL-SETTING EXAMPLE:

I will begin immediately to spend two hours a week visiting a home for the elderly, listening to lonely people, and chatting with them.

> *"There are those who enter the world in such poverty that they are deprived both of means and motivation to improve their lot. Unless they can be touched with the spark, which ignites the spirit of individual enterprise and determination, they will only sink into apathy, degradation and despair. It is for us who are more fortunate to provide that spark."*
>
> *– Agakhan IV*

49th hereditary imam,
Shi'a Ismaili Muslims

ADOPTING WELL-BALANCED HEALTH

> **A** *wise man should consider that health is the greatest of human blessings, and learn how by his own thought to derive benefit from his illnesses.*
>
> – Hippocrates

QUESTIONS TO PONDER:

▣ Am I participating in a fitness program that is enjoyable and sustainable?

▣ Do I have a short- and long-term goal for my financial freedom?

▣ Do I realize that positive thoughts are the seedlings of success?

▣ Do I have flexibility in my schedule for the people I care about?

▣ Do I realize it's not what I have but who ! have in my life that counts?

▣ Do I live a congruent life? Do I love life as a whole, or just some isolated parts?

▣ Do I feel a sense of fulfillment and wonder?

SUCCESS = BALANCE

We define success with one word: balance. When

you are spiritually, physically, socially, economically, and intellectually balanced, you have success. Life is like a jigsaw puzzle, with lots of different pieces in lots of different areas. Only when you place all the pieces on the board in their proper places is the jigsaw puzzle completed. So it is with life. If you excel in one or two areas but lag in others, you won't receive the satisfaction and fulfillment that you might otherwise receive.

We all have many different needs that must be met to achieve a healthy balance in life. We need to be healthy in body, mind, and spirit. So well-balanced health embraces your spiritual, physical, mental, emotional, and social needs. Leading a balanced life means taking a synergistic approach to meeting these different needs. To neglect one is to neglect the other.

Well-balanced thinking allows you to make decisions that take into account the overall good. It enables you to assess the consequences to your body, mind, and spirit. You are synergistic and integrated. You avoid segmented thinking. You realize that your body, mind, and spirit are interconnected; they all belong to you. You think in terms of integration and harmony. You are aware of interdependence, and see things in perspective. You are aware of your emotional, financial, physical, social, and spiritual needs. And you seek intentional congruence among them all.

In this chapter, we show you how to achieve well-balanced health, and explain why it is important to do so. We cover the following:

▨ What it means to be healthy.

▨ How health contributes to Life Balance.

▨ Practical strategies for living healthy

WHAT IT MEANS TO BE HEALTHY

The human body is a complex mechanism that requires great care and nourishment. When your health is not up to par, it affects all the other areas of your life. Physical well-being can be achieved by charting out a fitness plan that works for you. It should encompass three parts: aerobic fitness, muscle strengthening, and flexibility.

Aerobic conditioning improves the functions of your heart and lungs and increases the amount of oxygen delivered to your muscles. This, in turn, increases the amount of work your muscles can do. Muscle strengthening allows you to do more work and to be able to work for longer periods without getting tired. Flexibility is a result of physical activity. It comes from stretching. It helps reduce stiffness, fatigue, and pain that can be caused by stress and other related factors.

Health has many components – physical, mental, emotional, financial, and spiritual. Living a balanced life means balancing your time in terms of your relationships, work, spirituality, and the managing of your body and resources. Your physical health and finances are integral parts of your personal resources and need to be managed well. Without good health, it is hard to enjoy happiness. Without financial independence, you may experience stress that could lead to family breakdowns. All these bear a vital relationship to Life Balance.

HOW HEALTH CONTRIBUTES TO LIFE BALANCE

In this section we discuss the following:

▨ Physical Health.

▨ Financial Health.

▨ Mental Health.

▨ Emotional Health.

▨ Spiritual Health.

PHYSICAL HEALTH

You may feel too tired to exercise, but this is the only way to get rid of your fatigue and increase productivity and effectiveness. Exercise will clear your mind as well as build your strength. It does not necessarily cost a lot. It could be as simple as going for a walk or jogging. Swimming is a good low-impact exercise, and an aerobics video can be useful for exercising in the comfort and convenience of your home. Many local community centers run good gyms and sports centers, and classes are quite inexpensive. Joining a regular exercise class or getting involved in a team sport could also give some structure to your life. It's a good way to meet new people.

If you have a busy lifestyle, you may end up eating junk food because it's convenient. Eating healthy foods will stop you from bingeing on junk food, and it will help if you are gaining weight. A balanced diet means making sure you eat a variety of healthy foods without relying too much on sugary or fatty foods.

An active lifestyle coupled with a well-balanced diet will leave you feeling energized all day long. A well-balanced diet would include plenty of grains, minerals, and fiber, and lots of water, but low doses of sugar, saturated fats, and cholesterol.

It's important to incorporate physical activity into your daily life. Research shows that physical inactivity can cause premature death, chronic disease and disability. There are many pleasant ways to be active every day of the year – at home, at work, and within your community.

Some tips for a healthy lifestyle:

- Cultivate good dietary habits.

- Avoid the "work out-pig out" mentality.

- Get both exercise and rest.

- Work and relax: Give yourself a regular break to rejuvenate.

- Follow good sleep habits – not too much or too little. Nowadays, most people are sleep deprived. Power naps help.

- Avoid drugs, alcohol, and tobacco.

Taking care of yourself means investing in yourself, using whatever resources you have. If you feel the need to improve your health, consider getting more exercise and improving your diet. By setting yourself small goals, such as eating a piece of fruit each day, drinking an extra couple of glasses of water, or just taking a 20-minute daily walk, you can make a big difference in the way you feel.

The practice of yoga helps toward physical health as well as psychological well-being and spirituality. Through yoga, you have the potential to integrate all aspects of your being, including your physical, mental, emotional, and spiritual dimensions. Yoga improves your posture and alignment. The breathing practices provide the link between mind and body and provide release of tension and reduction of stress.

FINANCIAL HEALTH

"Wealth, like a tree, grows from a tiny seed," wrote George S. Clason, American author and financial-planning adviser. "The first copper you save is the seed from which your tree of wealth shall grow."

Many people in North America do not give due attention to their financial affairs. Roger and Rebecca Merrill, in their wonderful book, *Life Matters,* say that "giving finance a half-hearted gloss-over" is not enough for achieving financial success. Yet, financial stability is a very important part of a healthy, balanced life.

One of the gifts you can give to others, including your loved ones and the less privileged, is money. Money is an important commodity in our society. It provides for food, shelter, education, transportation, and health services. Money is attracted to those who value money and manage it well.

Good financial management results from saving, self-discipline, and proper planning. We know of some people with meager incomes who are debt-free, while others, who earn substantially more, are deep in debt. It's not how much we make that matters; it's how much we keep.

To make sound financial decisions, whether they are about savings for the future or making investments in stocks, you need to prepare a financial plan. You'll sleep better at night knowing that you and your family will be financially secure if calamity strikes.

Financial planning is essential for most people to get ahead financially. The basic process of financial planning involves setting financial goals, periodically reviewing your net worth, preparing budgets and debt-reduction plans, and looking at insurance, retirement, and tax planning.

Forming a habit of saving is vital. Ideally, at least 10% of your gross income should either go into forced savings or be invested wisely. The best way to do that is to have the money automatically deducted from your pay and put into savings before you even see it. Money spent on good financial advice is well spent.

Some tips to help with financial planning:

⊠ The Universe is abundant; therefore think and invite abundance.

⊠ Your diamonds are not in faraway mountains or in distant seas; they're in your own backyard, if you persist in looking for them.

⊠ Networks determine your net worth, so broaden your network.

⊠ What gets rewarded gets done, so reward yourself for small financial accomplishments.

⊠ Make money while you are asleep: Find passive investment.

⊠ Buy appropriate real estate and wait.

⊠ Prepare detailed marketing plans.

⊠ Kindle a burning desire to succeed financially.

⊠ Look at finances from the perspective of lifetime value. Every dollar is like a seed with lifetime value.

What George Clason prescribed in his classic, _The Richest man in Babylon_, is still quite valid:

- Fatten your purse.

- Control expenditures.

- Make your gold multiply.

- Guard against loss.

- Make dwelling a profitable investment.

- Ensure future incomes.

- Invest in what you know; seek professional advice.

It's simple, but it works. Good health and financial security are important elements in the achievement of balance and harmony in your life. People who let the love of money drive their lives may end up wealthy but unhappy. People who use money to accomplish positive achievement lead rich and rewarding lives. As circus tycoon P. T. Barnum put it, "Money is in some respects like fire: It is a very excellent servant but a terrible master."

As their children grew up, Nido and his wife, Mariana, would take them for a month's vacation every summer. At places such as Disney World, the children would constantly ask for more money to buy souvenirs and toys. It occurred to Nido and Mariana that the best thing to do was simply to give them a certain amount of money at the start of the vacation and let them buy what they wanted or, if they preferred, allow them just to keep the money. Nido began to notice that his children started to exercise a greater skill in decision-making. One day at a souvenir shop at Disney World, he noticed something remarkable. His two youngest children, then 7 and 4, were conspiring in the corner. He watched as they picked up one stuffed animal and paid the cashier for it. When Nido asked what they were up to, they told him they had decided they would simply pool their money and buy just one Teddy bear. They had agreed that one of them could use the bear on Monday, Wednesday, and Friday; the other one could use it on Tuesday, Thursday, and Saturday. The Teddy bear could rest on Sunday. The young children had learned a lesson about balancing their wants, their needs, and their budgetary constraints. It was a lesson Nido believes will serve them well in their adult lives.

Nido does not give his children pocket money. They have to earn it, based on performance and results – at school. So, for example, an "A" at the end of a semester would earn a $100 reward. A "B" earned only $75. A "C" brought no reward, because "C" is average and Nido doesn't reward mediocrity. He believes we should never reinforce behavior we don't want to see repeated. A child bringing home a "D" would owe Nido $50.

The Qubein children usually made "A's" and were wise enough to save their money and invest it in the stock market.

When it was their own hard-earned money, they extracted greater meaning from it and committed themselves to better planning.

MENTAL HEALTH

Researchers have found that your brain can produce substances that improve your physical health. The brain produces endorphins – natural painkillers – and interferon, which combats infections, viruses, and even cancer. The substances that your brain produces depend in part on your thoughts, feelings, expectations and attitudes. A positive attitude or expectation helps the brain to combat a disease more effectively. Spiritual well-being is also essential in helping you overcome personal challenges and circumstances beyond your control. Visualization, affirmations, and imagination also play vital roles in meeting life's challenges and keeping good mental health.

Just as the universe always seeks equilibrium, so does your body. Your internal conditions, such as blood pressure and body temperature, are maintained despite variations from external forces. As cells die, other cells replace them. It happens so naturally that we are completely unaware of the process. However, to maintain balance between mental and physical states, we need a strong sense of awareness.

Mental health involves regular inputs of inspiring material through reading, listening, and discussions in book clubs or at seminars. Spiritual health needs regular doses of meditation, prayers, and contribution, whereas emotional health needs effective communication and love.

EMOTIONAL HEALTH

Relationships, especially close ones with your spouse, children, parents, friends, and colleagues, need to be maintained and nurtured.

After years of studying human behavior, psychotherapist Carl Rogers believed strongly that all people, given the opportunity, could grow toward healthy maturity. Our relationships are decisive factors in experiencing this opportunity.

As we get older and experience more of life's quirks and twists, our choices and our values can either support relationships or destroy them. Spousal relationships are especially crucial to the achievement of maturity. And to have a good relationship with your spouse, it's essential that you spend personal time together.

Nido and Azim both schedule weekly private time with their wives that help keep their communication channels open and their relationships strong.

When Nido was 3 years old, his father fell sick and continued in poor health until his death three years later. Therefore, Nido grew up without a father. He did not get to play ball with his dad, or watch movies with him, or sit on his lap. He was never able to sit down with his dad at the end of the day and discuss the things he had done. He never got a goodnight kiss from his father. He knows the value of what he lost, and has been careful to make up to his own children what was lacking in his early life.

Nido's mother, Victoria Qubein, taught him that "Out of adversity beauty emerges." Relationships with family provide a strong sense of foundation for emotional health. Nido says that without his mother he would be nothing. She taught him all his principles. The sound relationship between mother and son provided an important ingredient in Nido's success and provided him with emotional strength.

Azim Regularly tucks his 9-year-old son into bed. Invariably, Tawfiq wants to hear funny stories before he goes to sleep, and he prefers unique and original tales. Azim combines philosophy and humor to transmit valuable lessons to his son while they share quality time together. Azim's wife, Farzana, has to remind them when it's past bedtime. When this happens, Azim and Tawfiq go hush until she disappears. Then they resume their time together until Tawfiq has laughed enough and dozes off, or Azim dozes off after exhausting his stories.

THE IMPORTANCE OF GOOD MENTAL AND EMOTIONAL HEALTH

Your mental and emotional health is as important as your physical health. Your body, mind, and heart are interconnected. When you have problems with one, the others are affected.

Some things we can do to produce well- rounded health:

▨ Cultivate the ability to enjoy life, to laugh and have fun.

▨ Take total responsibility for your life; avoid blaming others.

▨ Bounce back from problems – learn to deal with life's stresses.

▨ Pursue self-realization – participating in life to the fullest extent possible through meaningful activities and positive relationships.

▨ Develop the ability to change and grow as you experience a range of feelings and circumstances in your life.

▨ Apply a sense of balance in your life – between solitude and sociability, work and play, sleep and wakefulness, rest and exercise.

▨ Cultivate a sense of all-round excellence, with attention to mind, body, spirit, creativity, intellectual development, health, and other aspects of your life.

▨ Acquire the ability to care for yourself and for others.

▨ Develop self-confidence and good self-esteem.

▨ Recognize your self worth; you are a bundle of potential.

▨ Put things in perspective.

▨ Be patient.

▨ Strike a balance between boldness and prudence, rashness and wisdom.

▨ Acquire a sense of humor; learn to laugh at yourself.

When you take care of your emotional well-being, you will also connect with your spirituality and will become well balanced in this respect too.

EMOTIONAL INTELLIGENCE

Emotions tell you more about you than your mind does. When you observe emotions, you come to know more about yourself. But many people are not aware of their emotions. They lack emotional intelligence.

Daniel Goleman's book, _Emotional Intelligence_, tells why this quality can matter more than IQ. People with great IQs but not much emotional intelligence don't go very far in life. Great leaders, healthy family members, and balanced individuals possess a healthy dose of emotional intelligence, even though their IQs may not be spectacular.

Emotional intelligence includes self-awareness, self-discipline, and empathy. Goleman explains that when you recognize your feelings and are able to monitor and navigate through them, you become a better manager of your life.

Great leaders are able to channel their emotions in the service of a goal or purpose. Thus, they're able to motivate themselves. A relationship with family, colleagues, friends, and others is at the heart of balanced living. Understanding others' feelings and viewing things from their perspective opens the way for healthier relationships.

Those who can control their impulses and manage emotions in others tend to enjoy the best relationships. The real art of communication is distinguishing between what someone says and does and your own reactions to it or judgment on it. People often substitute anger for rational responses. Anger causes a lot of strife at home and at work. It is an out-of-control emotion. Your ability to monitor your feelings allows you to avoid putting yourself at its mercy. Goleman further explains that emotional intelligence hinges on the link between sentiment, character, and moral instincts.

Emotional intelligence promotes job security. Personality problems are at the root of most firings. Practical intelligence leads to people skills, which are a great asset today. So we need both.

"I'll pay for people's ability to get along with others more than any other skill," said Charles Schwab, founder of the financial-services firm that bears his name.

SPIRITUAL HEALTH

Although the spiritual side seems less relevant to many people, it is in fact the source of all health. It is the inside, which triggers the outside. The strength of the inside is the root that keeps all else firm. Therefore, value the intangibles, cultivate a sense of wonderment, turn your imagination loose, cultivate a sense of place in time, accumulate your memories, pursue happiness, involve yourself in the arts, and keep a positive, open mind. This will keep you young.

Look beyond the superficial. Happiness is not the same as having a ball or partying all the time. The Golden Rule, enunciated by Jesus in his Sermon on the Mount, advises: "Do unto others as you would have them do to unto you." This is where inner happiness comes from.

MAKE THE RIGHT CHOICES

The choices you make influence your well-rounded health. Do you choose to eat well and live an active life? Do you choose wisely between play and work; solitude and sociability; sleep and wakefulness; rest and exercise; caring for self and caring for others?

When you face up to your fears, they disappear. When you avoid blaming others and take full responsibility, you bring positive change into your life. You have the choice, and as you exercise this choice you create your destiny.

Audrey was struggling to achieve well-rounded health. After being guided at one of our sessions, she took these steps:

▣ Three or four times a week, she engaged in the 20:20:20 Hour of Power, devoting 20 minutes to exercise, 20 minutes to meditation, and 20 minutes to uplifting reading.

■ During her 20 minutes of exercise, she listened to motivational sessions.

■ She began multi tasking by taking separate walks with her husband and her teen-age child twice a week.

These three activities gave her a head start toward her goal of more balanced health. Sometimes small changes create big results.

Affirm that you appreciate well-rounded health. Acknowledge what is working in your life. Visualize excellent all-round health. All these techniques work. They are explained in Chapter 10, "Practicing Enlightened Persistence."

How successful you are in your relationships, the kind of success you achieve, and the financial security you attain all stem from how centered you are in your life. By keeping your life centered on correct principles, you create a solid foundation for the development of your life-support systems. You are then able to encompass and integrate the truly important areas of your life. What does it all have to do with well-rounded health? Living with integrity and congruence gives you the much-needed vigor and health.

"People with greater certainty about their feelings are better pilots of their lives," Daniel Goleman assures us.

SUMMARY:

In summary, you move toward adopting well-balanced health when you do the following:

■ (1) Live an active life. Have an exercise regime. Get enough rest and eat a balanced diet. Avoid alcohol, tobacco, or other drugs, and limit your caffeine intake.

▓ (2) Start your financial planning early in life. Prepare your financial goals, including net worth, cash flow, and an automatic savings plan.

▓ (3) Keep a positive attitude. Make a list of the things that are troubling you; then fold it and put it away for the rest of the day.

▓ (4) Prioritize your challenges, and deal with the ones that are most stressful.

▓ (5) Do something that is fun and relaxing for you (go to a funny movie, take a walk on the beach, listen to music, read a good book, or talk to a friend).

▓ (6) Be sure to spend ample time with people whose company you enjoy, generally those who have upbeat and positive attitudes.

▓ (7) Attend to your spiritual needs by meditating or praying, or by appreciating a beautiful sunset.

YOUR GOAL-SETTING EXERCISE

CHAPTER VIII: ADOPTING WELL BALANCED HEALTH

What areas in your life do you need to work on to adopt well-balanced health? Ask yourself what one big obstacle is getting in the way of your achieving well-balanced health? Set your goal and timeline to overcome this obstacle.

My goal is to work on the following areas in terms of maintaining my holistic health:

....

....

....

I commit the following timelines to implement this habit

....

....

....

If I follow through with this goal it will make a significant difference to my balanced living.

GOAL-SETTING EXAMPLE:

I will go for a half hour brisk walk five times a week commencing next week.

> *"Know the Self to be sitting in the chariot, the body to be the chariot, the intellect the charioteer, and the mind the reins."*
>
> – The Upanishads

UNDERSTANDING THE TIME MYTH

One of the most tragic things I know about human nature is that all of us tend to put off living. We are all dreaming of some magical rose garden over the horizon – instead of enjoying the roses that are blooming outside our windows today.

– Dale Carnegie

QUESTIONS TO PONDER:

▣ Is my time spent in alignment with my purpose?

▣ Am I organized and methodical? Do I have effective systems in place?

▣ Do I manage time or does time manage me?

▣ Do I realize that the most important gift I can give my family is my time?

▣ Do I realize that sometimes slow is fast when it comes to relationships?

▣ Do I find that the harder I work, the more there is to do?

▣ Do I plan and use my most productive time to do the most productive work?

MEASURING TIME BY THE BREATH

Time is life and life is time. Your life is measured by the number of breaths you take. Every breath reduces the inventory available to you. If Life Balance is important to you, then you can achieve it by managing yourself and your time.

You are blessed with time to live, but how do you value this time? Time is yours. It is a great gift. To get maximum benefit from it, you must reflect on how to spend it and how to make appropriate choices. The way you spend your time can create either balance or imbalance. You are on your way to Life Balance when you learn to differentiate between *chronos* (linear time) and *kairos* (quality or value time).

Chronos is the Greek word for time as we measure it by clocks and calendars. *Kairos* is the Greek word used in the Christian Bible to indicate a fixed or definite period – an opportune season or a critical time.

When you have Life Balance, you find ways to spend more of your life in *Kairos*.

If you are like many busy people whom we have encountered in our professional careers, you probably feel that your biggest challenge to achieving Life Balance is lack of time.

The purpose of this chapter is to illustrate that lack of time is not the real problem; the problem is failure to manage life and time.

People are always saying, "I haven't got time." Remove those words from your vocabulary. If you think you don't have enough time, you'll act in harmony with your thoughts, and your thoughts will become self-fulfilling prophecy. We all have 24 hours every day – 86,400 seconds to spend on the things we value. That's lots of time. If you think you don't have enough time, you need to examine the way you're spending your time. How you spend your time is a choice you can make.

In this section we recommend that you do the following:

▦ Develop a purpose-oriented time-management system.

▦ Be organized and methodical.

A PURPOSE-ORIENTED TIME MANAGEMENT SYSTEM

The first step in developing a purpose-oriented time-management system is to identify a purpose. Don't wait for chance to nudge you toward your destiny. Choose the destiny you want, and use your time and choices to take you to it.

In Chapter One, we learned the importance of choosing our destiny through creation of a vision and the establishment of goals leading toward the vision. Review your vision and mission daily so you can use your goals as the basis for managing your time. This way you can plan your time and activities based on the way they help you in meeting your goals. You need to schedule your priorities and not just prioritize what is already in your schedule.

When you've established your priorities, every job, meeting, phone call or e-mail becomes a goal-driven exercise. Constantly ask yourself: "If this doesn't advance me toward my goals, then why should I do it?"

The key to success in time management and self-management is to operate around a tight set of priorities. Many people are urgency-driven as opposed to being purpose-driven. Generally, what is important is not urgent, unless you have neglected it and allowed it to become urgent. Being proactive will help you spend your time on important areas of your life.

When you have a purpose-oriented time-management system, you are managing your life. You know what is most important to you, and you make choices that are aligned to your purpose. You are devoting your energies to things that have your highest priority. You are balancing spontaneity and planning to achieve optimum results. You analyze the way your time is being spent, so you know whether it is aligned to your purpose. You are able to eliminate things that are not important to you, thus creating additional time for things that matter most.

In this section we give key pointers on how to:

⊞ Balance spontaneity and planning to achieve optimum results.

⊞ Analyze the way your time is being spent.

⊞ Prepare a "stop-doing" list.

⊞ Apply your energies to things that are your highest priority.

⊞ Achieve behavioral economics and discipline.

BALANCE YOUR SPONTANEITY WITH PLANNED ACTION

Planning is a great way to get things done and to be on target. Otherwise you can be running around chasing rabbits and not accomplishing much. Planning lets you consolidate your work and merge similar tasks, thereby using less energy. It enables you to sequence your activities to ensure a productive outcome. For example, if you use your evening to plan for the next day, you can wake up ready for immediate action. Nido keeps all the clothes he plans to wear ready for the next day; he doesn't want to wake up in the morning and use his prime time to worry about what he is going to wear. Most of us underestimate the time it takes to do things. Through planning and evaluation, you can schedule a realistic amount of time in your scheduling. Planning can also help create systems, which are excellent in creating leverage.

But if you operate *everything* by plan, you may miss out on some rare and precious moments. The best business ideas often come from unplanned conversations. You may meet people unexpectedly at restaurants during business luncheons, or bump into them at the supermarket. Never ignore previous acquaintances; they could be useful sources of new ideas for increasing your business. Spontaneity should never be considered a waste of time, even for people who just "don't have the time."

Too much structure or too much going with the flow can be counter-productive. It is the balance between the two that creates balance in your life.

SOME PRACTICAL TIPS:

- Make planned calls.
- Avoid small talk.
- Allow flexibility.
- Don't allow people to throw their problems at you.

⊠ Work off-site.

⊠ Stand up while talking on the telephone, and you will find that you're much more focused and to the point. Your voice will also convey that you are busy.

⊠ Strike a balance between "no interruptions" and some important interruptions.

ANALYZE THE WAY YOUR TIME IS BEING SPENT

"Dost thou love life?" asked Benjamin Franklin. "Then do not squander your time, for that is the stuff life is made of."

Life and time are one and the same. What gets measured gets improved, so making a budget of your time and analyzing where it is going can significantly improve your efficiency. Preparing a weekly time budget helps you to balance your activities better. Prepare a budget of your time, identifying how much time you wish to spend each week on each of the key areas in your life. The total time should add up to 168 hours.

Find out how much time you're devoting to work, study, meetings, exercise, relaxation, sleep, family, shopping, and other events. Keep a detailed list for a week or a month. Next, give yourself a set of priorities and see how you can provide time for the most important things in your life. For one month, summarize the areas in which you spend your time. Evaluate the quality of the time you spend in each. Analyze the variance between the way you spend your time and the way you want to spend it, and take corrective action.

Beware of getting caught up too much in *chronos* – the quantitative aspect of managing time – and losing the essential value of the exercise. So in your evaluation, look for not only the quantity of time spent in each of your core areas but also the quality of the results you have produced in these areas. A watch is a useful thing, but it can become a hindrance. Relationships with loved ones are infinitely more important than the clock, which does not measure *kairos* – quality time. When planning, expect things to come up that you did not anticipate. Some of these may be important. Therefore, allow some flexibility in the planning process to incorporate these opportunities or occurrences.

To paraphrase a popular adage among management experts, "What gets measured gets improved." When you measure the way you spend your time, you are bound to improve your use of time. Invest time in areas that are your highest priorities. Give everything you have to these priorities and watch yourself progress. When you have less on your plate, you invite integrity and harmony into your life. But this "less" is more, because it is on your highest priority list. Why exert yourself to do brilliantly what you don't have to do at all?

Azim has a habit of budgeting his weekly time between family and work. He also keeps track of where he spends his time. This allows him to be effective with his time. By budgeting 28 hours a week for his family, he is able to spend time with his loved ones. Also, by writing in his journal, he is able to ensure that he gives them not just a quantity of time but time infused with quality of interaction and bonding. He regards this as a great gift to his family.

The quality of interaction is more important than

quantity, so one cannot measure everything based on time alone. However, well-measured quantities create room for quality to manifest itself. A half-hour saved daily amounts to about 180 hours per year, which is equivalent to four weeks of full-time work.

PREPARE A 'STOP-DOING' LIST

Less is more. Doing fewer important things is far better than wading through a bigger list of unimportant things. Thus focus on "undoing" your list rather than on adding to it.

If you learn to turn down unimportant tasks, it will enable you to focus on high-priority work. Don't sweat the unimportant tasks. Focus on important things such as your health, family relationships, or finances. A major setback in one of those areas could be disastrous.

Practice behavior that leads to optimum results. Just as you would invest your money for optimum returns, you should invest your time in areas that will bring you the best return. That means turning down activities that yield minimal benefits.

This strategy also works for great companies. In his book, _From Good to Great,_ Jim Collins explains that good-to-great companies do not principally focus on what to do to become great. They focus equally on what not to do and what to stop doing.

APPLY YOUR ENERGY WHERE YOUR PRIORITY IS HIGHEST

Very few of us can call ourselves high-energy and high-focus people. Here's why: Such people are the ones who take the time to plan, to prioritize, and to stick to their plans. They pick their battles with care, not wasting time on petty issues. They don't wait for someone else to make things happen for them. They don't allow e-mails, telephone calls, or other interruptions to become distractions; they set aside a special time for these distractions each day and spend the rest of the day in more productive pursuits. They encourage their teams to take responsibility for themselves, so that they are not constantly called upon as arbiters or firefighters. They take time to reflect and to plan ways to recharge themselves, so that they are refreshed for every new project.

At certain times in your day, you may notice a trend toward diminishing returns. That's the signal to switch to some other way of spending your time. You might go for a walk or turn to some important activity requiring a different mindset and energy. This will keep you from getting bogged down in the Law of Diminishing Returns.

BEHAVIORAL ECONOMICS AND DISCIPLINE

Behavioral economics decrees that for every behavior you display, there must be economic benefit. You must get something in return. This calls for focus and authenticity.

If you're not focused, your efforts will be diffused over many different endeavors. You may be a good time manager, but you'll never be as high a performer or as productive a leader as when you are focused. You focus on the most important thing, and you find that the other small things take care of themselves. Having a focus is a byproduct of purpose. The clearer your purpose in life, the more focused you will be on the areas that are really important in your life. Once you're focused, you'll know which areas to delegate, which areas to throw completely out the window, and which areas to give your best resources.

Be a disciplined worker. Figure out which parts of the day are the really creative hours for you. For example, early in the morning is Nido's most creative time. That's when he does his writing and thinking. He has all his meetings in the afternoon, because it's less productive for him.

Discipline is a big point for service providers, especially for entrepreneurs. Entrepreneurs have no bosses to watch over them or make sure that they are getting their jobs done. They have to be their own bosses. They have to supervise their own behavior. Part of their discipline is to believe firmly in behavioral economics – that every behavior they display must produce economic benefit.

To achieve this level of productivity requires authenticity. You don't become successful by doing the right things. You become successful by being the right person. Who you are leads to what you do, not the other way around. That's what authenticity is all about. It comes from within the person, so to achieve it we have to work on the inner person, not the outward actions.

Congruence is a big piece of authenticity. The word refers to harmony of actions. Your actions in all your endeavors must harmonize the way the notes from a variety of instruments harmonize to create a symphony – a pleasing whole.

If you have congruence in your life, then what you say, how you think, and they way you act, all come together to make a complete, harmonious picture.

Sometimes you may do things to contribute to good causes that produce no economic benefits to you. But here, too, you must assess whether you are using your time effectively and efficiently to produce the results you set out to produce and provide the maximum benefit to those you are trying to help.

BE ORGANIZED AND METHODICAL

Being organized and methodical will enable you to manage time with maximum efficiency. Combined with the purpose-oriented time-management system, you'll be able to achieve effectiveness and efficiency, which promote Life Balance. In this section we cover the following points:

▨ Do the most important thing first thing in the morning.

▨ Don't shuffle papers; make quick decisions.

▨ Avoid interruptions.

▨ Delegate effectively.

▨ Use deadlines to create results.

▨ Do just one thing at a time, finishing it before you move to the next thing.

▨ Be decisive.

▨ Be organized through effective systems.

START THE DAY WITH THE MOST IMPORTANT THINGS

If you want important stuff done, schedule it. If you want it done most efficiently, schedule it for first thing in the morning.

Instead of prioritizing what is on your "to-do" list, prepare a list of your priorities using your goals as a starting point. It's all too common to use "I don't have time" as an excuse for avoiding the important things, such as exercise, reading, planning, and family time. If you schedule important work, it gets done. If you schedule it first thing in the morning, it gets done best.

Azim caters to his need for meditation, reading, and walking first thing in the morning, to give him a head start on his day. The first hour of the day sets the tone for the rest of the day. It's the time when your energy levels are at their highest, so use it to do your highest-priority work. Make sure you get a good night's rest before tackling your early-morning tasks. That will help you start your day with a bang instead of a yawn.

Let the first hour of your day be your hour of power. Get that exhilarating feeling that rewards work well done. Make sure you attend to the most difficult tasks. You'll find that the rest of the day will be much more productive and upbeat.

Stephen Covey and Roger and Rebecca Merrill, in their book, *First Things First,* talk about subordinating the clock to the compass. This empowers you to shift the focus from the urgent to the important.

DON'T SHUFFLE PAPERS; MAKE QUICK DECISIONS

Some people waste a lot of time deciding what to do with the paper that flows across their desks. When you look at a paper for the first time, make a decision to act on it right away. If you are unsure about something in a communication, remember that the time to decide is now, based on the present time and situation. When you start reading through things, you have the momentum to decide right away what you want to do with it. Be ruthless with clutter, and don't file away papers that can either be dealt with or thrown away. This simple exercise will keep you from dealing repeatedly with the same piece of paper.

AVOID INTERRUPTIONS

Every interruption is a big time drainer. Some interruptions are valuable. For example, when your child wants to bond with you or your aging parents need you to take them to the doctor, don't put it off till later. But many interruptions are nothing more than time wasters. Beware of them; they can exhaust your energy while achieving nothing. Don't get ruffled every time you're interrupted. Just stick to your plan, based on key priorities.

Use e-mails to communicate instantly with clients or business connections, but don't allow your email to become an alternative mailing address. If you have a private e-mail account to which fewer than a dozen people have access, you're less likely to spend hours going through all the messages directed to you.

The notion that you must be "connected" at all times is completely invalid. Car phones and beepers are major deterrents to your focus. They're also safety hazards.

DELEGATE EFFECTIVELY

Good leaders delegate effectively. The key to delegation is to communicate clearly to avoid any misunderstanding. Meeting with others to plan your work creates buy-in and better understanding from the people you are delegating to. Encouraging people to be result-oriented as opposed to problem-oriented improves productivity. If you are delegating to your team and you notice signs of non-commitment, confront the problem immediately. There's a big difference between deciding to jump and thinking about jumping. Commitment means jumping. If you want to be effective in delegating, get commitment first.

USE DEADLINES TO CREATE RESULTS

Deadlines create momentum. People who work under deadlines tend to keep up the pace and to point their efforts toward the finish.

Here are some tips for accomplishing difficult or long-term tasks:

- Break the task into bite-sized segments.
- Delegate.
- Reward yourself after small accomplishments.
- Share specialized help.
- Create milestones.
- Get started.
- Keep going.

Therefore, if you find that you are postponing some important work, set yourself some mini-deadlines and get going.

Procrastination can be a time-killer. We usually procrastinate when we're uncertain, or find the work ahead of us difficult or unpleasant. The key is to get started, even if it's doing nothing more than taking the file out onto your desk and writing a heading. Once you get started, you create a momentum for yourself.

Another good way to get started is to spend time planning and organizing. Another possibility is to delegate the task to someone more qualified to do the work.

Some matters should be deferred until a later time. When matters of low priority and low importance are clamoring for your attention while you're confronted with matters of high priority and importance, the less-important stuff should be relegated to the back of the line.

But actions that move you toward your goals should not be brushed aside with the promise that you'll get around to them "sooner or later."

As Nido put it: "Nothing gets accomplished 'sooner or later,' It gets accomplished at a specific time and specific place."[7]

COMPLETE ONE TASK BEFORE MOVING TO THE NEXT

Many people tend to jump from one task to another. That's the inefficient way of doing things. As you work on a task, you build momentum. When you drop it to take on a different task, you lose the momentum on the abandoned task, and you have to build up a head of steam on the new task. A habit of finishing the task you started creates efficiency. It allows you to sustain your momentum, and you get an extra boost from the satisfaction of seeing the task successfully accomplished. This extra boost will help you get started on the next task.

---

[7] Nido Qubein, The Time Is Now, the Person Is You (High Point, N.C., Executive Press, 1997) p. 77.

Leaving a job half-done can double the time it takes to finish it. Half-done work is worthless. To get a long-term job finished, create milestones on the road to completion and attain those milestones one at a time.

You've heard the admonition, "Do it right the first time." That's good advice. If you do the job wrong, you often must start over from the beginning and repeat a lot of the steps you did correctly before your goof. You'll save time by being slow and meticulous; you'll waste time by being fast and slipshod.

BE DECISIVE

"Sit, walk or run. Just don't wobble," goes an old Zen saying.

That's another way of saying, "Don't waffle; be decisive."

When you are decisive and totally focused on a task, you accomplish things much more quickly. Focused attention allows you to achieve more. It's your attitude of mind that counts. Say to yourself: "I have more than enough time for all I want to do," and you increase the possibilities. This attitude allows you to be decisive and not waste time. It also emboldens you with the conviction that the job can be done. When you approach a task with the conviction that you have more than enough time for everything else in your life, the task is likely to be completed much faster. You can focus better when you don't feel pressed for time, and this focus will add momentum to your progress.

BE ORGANIZED THROUGH EFFECTIVE SYSTEMS

Take the time to organize and create a system. People waste a lot of time looking for things. That time wasted could be used to create, to innovate, and to achieve balance by dedicating the time to areas that are important to you.

If things are done in proper sequence, they take less time. This sets the stage for important things to happen. Things just don't happen on their own. You have to plan what to do and schedule a time to do it. Allow enough time, but not so much that you end up filling it with trivial pursuits. It's easier to create solutions to well-defined problems, so budget time to define your problem. Having the right system gives you great leverage. Here are some useful tips for organizing your life and making it more effective:

▣ Set up a filing system to organize your paperwork. When papers are organized, they can be found more quickly. You feel in control of your life because you know where everything is. This organized system cuts down on unnecessary stress.

▣ Organize your travel time. When you organize your travel time, you can actually fit in a lot more things. You can catch up on reading, writing, telephone calls, naps, and listening to educational CDs or music.

▣ Organize your appointments by priority. This will allow you to give your greatest attention to the more important ones. Schedule your important appointments for the time of day when you're most rested and alert; schedule the less-important ones for the end of the day, when your energy level may be lower but can still handle low-priority tasks.

▣ Break large tasks into smaller steps. Sequencing avoids duplication and allows for a smoother ride through the task. Many of us avoid big projects either because we don't know where to begin or have limited time to complete them. But once you break the big projects into bite- sized tasks you are able to tackle the biggest jobs.

▧ Start with priority items.

▧ Group related activities that might be dealt with via e-mail.

▧ Make waiting time productive. For example, when you go to the dentist, carry work material in your jacket that takes a few minutes to complete, or take a book that you can browse through. Not only will this make your time productive; it may also take your mind off the drill.

▧ Stick to your schedule as far as possible. This will save time thinking about what to do next.

▧ Avoid unplanned activities.

▧ Schedule relaxing time.

▧ Organize your presentations. If you organize your notes in orderly files, you'll save lots of time when you have to make spur-of-the-moment presentations.

▧ Eliminate clutter. Why file away information that you don't need?

▧ De-clutter your space. Tidy up your car, desk, bedroom, and kitchen. This way you won't be bogged down trying to locate the things buried in the clutter.

▧ Write down your goals every morning. Writing helps crystallize your thoughts

Edward Deming, eminent American statistician, found that 94% of all failures result from flaws in the system, and not from somebody's unwillingness to do a good job. Take the time to set up and refine your system. Don't tell yourself you don't have enough time.

That's just an excuse. Making time is more efficient than making excuses. Get organized and create the additional time.

If you're having difficulty mastering the art of managing time and self, consider working with a mentor. Mentors can lead you to better ways to find the time to do all you want to do.

Humans are creatures of habit. Review your habits to see whether the way you do things is efficient and effective. Sometimes, by changing a routine task, you can save a chunk of time that you could be spending with a loved one or on essential reading.

Good time-management habits start at the top, with the leaders at workplaces or institutions. But those habits don't automatically trickle down.

They have to be planned for, cultivated, encouraged, and enforced, or they just won't become part of the larger system. Time is a crucial resource for any individual or organization. It's the most valuable resource, and it's non-renewable.

Besides managing your own time, you may find yourself in a position that calls for managing the time of everyone working for you. The better you become at it, the more successful you'll eventually become. You need to emphasize results, not activities. Bringing every task to closure as quickly as possible is a wonderful habit to cultivate and a good example for others.

These are a few examples of how different people manage their time:

Samantha — a great time manager but a poor life manager:

Everything for Samantha is structured. There is no room for flexibility or unplanned activities. This backfires for her. Life is uncharted territory. Sometimes great opportunities arise and are missed because of too much structure. Her teenage son wanted to open up to Samantha, but when he approached her it was not part of her structured time, so she put him off. When she finally found time to work him into her schedule, he was not in a mood to talk. The key is to allow some flexibility in your time management so that you can get on with life management. As Nido puts it, "Time management makes each minute count. Life management makes your whole existence count."

Life management is easier when you are clear on what's important to you. In this case, Samantha's son was very important to her. But her system wasn't flexible enough to allow this importance to influence her schedule. She could have made time to talk to her son. Good life management demanded that she do so.

Linda – a hard worker but not a good time manager or life manager.

Linda was always very tired, not accomplishing much in either her personal or her professional life. A lot of her time was wasted on intemptions. She was not very organized, so she was constantly looking for things and duplicating her work. Not a very good situation.

Arthur – a good life manager, but not a good time manager.

Arthur was always relaxed and went with the flow; he was good to be around. He got a lot done, because he swam with the current. There was no stress or tension. But Arthur was unable to deal with the important issues. He neglected his exercise, reading, and meditation, and rarely went one-on-one with those close to him.

Shirley — a good time manager and a good life manager

Shirley had a well-organized weekly schedule budgeted. She allowed enough flextime as well. This allowed room for interruptions if they were very important and were aligned with her mission or vision. She was able to combine Samantha's time-management and Arthur's life-management skills. A great combination; it's a choice worthy of emulation.

All of us have many roles and responsibilities. When we devote sufficient time to those we have identified as most important, we can create balance and harmony in your lives. In the fullest sense, balance is achieved when you harmonize body, mind, and soul. It is the fusion of the different facets of life that produces the synergy within you to achieve all sorts of great things.

SUMMARY:

In summary, you move toward understanding the time myth when you do the following:

▓ (1) Remember that you have lots of time – 86,400 seconds daily –to do things that you value.

⊠ (2) Use your time and choices consistently with the destiny you want.

⊠ (3) Have a purpose-oriented time-management system that does the following:

⊠ Balances spontaneity and planning to achieve optimum results.

⊠ Lets you analyze the way you spend your time.

⊠ Lets you prepare a 'stop doing' list.

⊠ Devotes your energies to things that are your highest priority

⊠ (4) Be organized and methodical by:

⊠ Doing the most important thing first thing in the morning.

⊠ Avoiding shuffling paper. This will prevent you from looking at the same paper several times.

⊠ Avoiding interruptions.

⊠ Practicing effective Delegation.

⊠ Using deadlines to create results.

⊠ Doing just one thing at a time to its completion before moving to the next thing.

⊠ Doing it now.

⊠ Being decisive, which creates momentum.

⊠ Being organized and creating a system.

YOUR GOAL-SETTING EXERCISE

CHAPTER IX: UNDERSTANDING THE TIME MYTH

What areas in your life do you need to work on to understand the time myth? Ask yourself: What is the one big obstacle getting in the way of my mastering time and life management? Set your goal and timeline to overcome this obstacle.

My goal is to work on the following areas in terms of managing my life and my time:

....

....

....

I commit to the following timelines to implement this habit:

....

....

....

If I follow through with this goal it will make a significant difference toward my balanced living.

GOAL-SETTING EXAMPLE:

I will organize my office room, filing cabinets and all my research material so I can easily find things I am looking for. I will complete this exercise by the end of this month.

"The unexamined life is not worth living."
                                                    – Socrates

Practicing Enlightened Persistence

Just remember that the greatest men in all history were the products of courage, and courage, you know, is born in the cradle of adversity.

— Napoleon Hill

QUESTIONS TO PONDER:

⊠ Do you believe that Life Balance is possible in your current circumstances?

⊠ Do you believe that balance is a choice you make?

⊠ Do you have faith and conviction that you can achieve the ideal balance you conceived for yourself?

⊠ What will happen to your balance when you meet with unexpected challenges, or pressing deadlines, or enormous change?

⊠ Do you regularly use affirmations, feeling, and conviction to invite balance?

⊠ Can you imagine and visualize what balance looks like to you?

▓ Do you display courage each time you encounter temporary defeat?

WELCOME CHALLENGES, OBSTACLES, AND HURDLES

You were born to succeed. The universe and your creator want you to succeed. You have been given the resources and capacity to succeed. You are encouraged to have Life Balance, and you can have Life Balance. If it is to be, it is up to you. But you can achieve Life Balance only after facing challenges, obstacles, and hurdles. You need them to increase your strength and resolve. So if you confidently look at your challenges as steppingstones, you will display enlightened persistence. This is important, because otherwise you will easily give up and will not achieve Life Balance.

You practice enlightened persistence when you realize that if you don't persist you won't succeed. If you don't succeed financially, at work, or in the family, Life Balance is affected. You therefore view persistence as a positive. You view challenges, obstacles, and hurdles as positive steps toward Life Balance.

If you have been implementing the strategies we've recommended in this book, keep it up. But don't despair if you're having trouble implementing them. Remember that challenges are blessings in disguise. They help you tap into your potential and your genius. How will you discover your talents and reserve strength without challenges and obstacles? Enlightened persistence will lead you to them. As the Roman poet Horace put it, "Adversity reveals genius."

And as Doug Weed said, "Goliath was the best thing that happened to David."

In this chapter, you'll learn that all worthwhile goals require effort and persistence. We'll explain:

■ What enlightened persistence is.

■ Why enlightened persistence is important, and what it has to do with Life Balance.

■ Strategies for practicing enlightened persistence.

WHAT IS ENLIGHTENED PERSISTENCE?

Enlightened Persistence means working with a sense of desire and conviction: the desire to achieve Life Balance and the conviction that you can reach it, despite all the challenges that arise.

Most of us miss our best opportunities because they come disguised as hard work. Hard work is a fact of life. If you want to be successful, you have to work hard. Thomas Edison was on the money when he remarked, "Genius is 1% inspiration and 99% perspiration."

But hard work doesn't have to be drudgery. It can be a source of great enjoyment. The writer of Ecclesiastes expressed it well: "There is nothing better for a man than that he should eat and drink, and that he should make his soul enjoy good in his labor."[8] ■

If you develop joy in your work, you'll find that it produces positive energy, which promotes balance. To develop joy in your work, you must be doing something that you're good at, that is meaningful to you, and that contributes to your family, your organization, and society.

---

[8] ■ The Holy Bible, Authorized Version, Ecclesiastes 2:24

The two of us have been successful as authors and speakers. For many people, that would be arduous, if not frightening work. The fear of public speaking is one of the most common phobias in the world. The task of putting down thoughts in writing is daunting to many people who are, nevertheless, very intelligent and creative. If you have that attitude toward speaking and writing, don't try to become a public speaker or an author. Find something you're good at and that you enjoy doing. There's something out there for everyone.

We find joy in speaking and writing because we love what we do. We can put an enormous amount of effort into it and yet remain energetic and centered. You can do the same in a field that you enjoy and are good at.

For many people, hard work is a drain on energy and emotions. They're tired and stressed out. Why? Because they are not focused on what they're good at, and they can't see their work as a benefit to their families, their organizations, and society.

Find the work that brings you joy. When you find it, pursue it with enlightened belief. Enlightened belief will lead to persistence, and persistence will make it happen.

OK, so it won't be easy. Both of us went through immense challenges to get to where we are now. Nido was a penniless teenager who couldn't speak English when he arrived in America. But he persisted because he was confident that anybody could succeed in America. His persistence enabled him to build his fortune on the art of communication in English.

Azim spent approximately 10,000 hours in his writing and speaking career before he could place his book in a bookstore. But he persisted because he knew he was going to make it, no matter what.

"You may have the loftiest goals, the highest ideals, and the noblest dreams," wrote Nido, "but remember this: Nothing works unless you *do* and persist in doing."

You display enlightened persistence when you have passion for what you do. When you love what you do, you work with gusto. Generally, this comes about when you align your work with your personal mission. You may need to do some soul-searching to discover your noble calling and purpose in life. In Chapter Three, we noted that meditation and reflection can help you discover your personal mission. By going into silence, you connect with your spirit and trigger your intuition and gut feeling – your sixth sense.

Enthusiasm is the positive inner force that makes things happen. It stems from a gracious persuasion and an excitement for life. The less-determined do only what is required of them, and sometimes less; but winners always do more than is required, and they do it with enthusiasm. Enthusiastic people experience life from the inside out and display inspiration, courage, creativity, and insight.

Most of us, to varying degrees, carry baggage from the past that hampers our future success. You must constantly remind yourself that your past failures in achieving Life Balance will not determine your future success. They just determine your starting point. Your future success will be based on your actions today.

You must have total belief in this for enlightened persistence to arise.

If your life has been unbalanced for a while, things will not change overnight. You will need to implement and persist in some of the strategies we recommend in this book. We suggest that you persist the enlightened way – having the knowledge and faith that your persistence will pay off. Without this belief and conviction, your persistence will carry no weight. But be aware that challenges and changes will come in your life. They will keep testing you and will keep changing the landscape. Here, again, you need to persist with enlightenment. Enlightened persistence comes with clarity, affirmations, imagination, and patience.

WHY ENLIGHTENED PERSISTENCE IS IMPORTANT

The clearer you are about what Life Balance looks like for you, and the more faith and conviction you have that you can achieve it, the more you invite it into your life. If you believe you can create the ideal Life Balance for yourself, you can attract that balance into your life. For example, you may feel that your week has been balanced if you are able to arrange the following:

⊠ An hour of one-on-one time twice a week with your spouse and each of the children.

⊠ A half-hour of exercise four to five times a week.

⊠ Four or five hours of reading a week.

⊠ A review of your financial plan.

⊠ Between 45 and 55 hours of work each week.

▓ A half-hour for meditation or silence four or five times a week.

▓ A half-hour for visualization four or five times a week.

▓ A relaxed outing with your family for at least 3 hours each weekend.

▓ Being relaxed and guided by your center at all times when things change and life throws you curve balls.

AFFIRMATIONS AND VISUALIZATIONS

Many people have told us that affirmations and visualizations can lead to success. They can also invite Life Balance. Affirm daily that your life is in harmony and that you have achieved balance amid change and chaos. Visualize the ideal situation along with your reactions, your outlook, and your attitude in the bustle of life. Watch how favorably you respond to your challenges.

The law of attraction says that what you want, believe, and desire strongly is attracted to you, and the stronger the desire and belief, the better the chances of attraction. So here are the daily affirmations you might make, on rising and on retiring, to bring about the balanced week we outlined:

▓ I meet my spouse and each of the children twice a week for at least an hour.

▓ I exercise for a half-hour at least four or five times a week.

▓ I read four or five hours a week.

▓ I review my financial plan for at least an hour every week.

▓ I work between 45 and 55 hours a week.

▓ I meditate for at least a half-hour four or five days a week.

▓ I relax for at least three hours every weekend with my family.

▓ I feel relaxed and guided by my center, even when things change and life throws curve balls.

STRATEGIES FOR PRACTICING ENLIGHTENED PERSISTENCE

Now let's discuss these strategies for practicing enlightened persistence:

▓ Affirmations.

▓ Imagination.

▓ Feeling and allowing.

▓ Unexpected challenges.

▓ Temporary defeats.

▓ Belief in yourself.

▓ Courage.

▓ Trust and faith.

AFFIRMATIONS

Affirmations are positive thoughts that you feed yourself. They create energy, passion, and gusto. They are the catalysts that create action and overcome inertia and self-doubt. Don't let doubt come into this. A small doubt grows like a seedling. Things will not change overnight. It will take time, but you have to display enlightened persistence. This means you persist because you know that it will pay off; there's no doubt in your mind about it. When the will comes into conflict with the imagination, the imagination invariably carries the day.

"A feeble man can see the farms that are fenced and tilled," wrote philosopher-poet Ralph Waldo Emerson. "The strong man sees the possible houses and farms. His eyes make estates as fast as the sun breeds clouds."

Visualize a week that incorporates meditation, one-on-one visits with your spouse and children, exercise, reading, review of your financial plan and any necessary corrective action, work, relaxing time, and the feeling of being centered despite variances and challenges.

If you do imagination and visualization exercises often, you will invite the feeling of victory. You will see what Life Balance looks like, and you'll be able to attract it into your life.

IMAGINATION

"If you can dream it, you can do it," Walt Disney said.

Affirmations unleash our imagination. Once you have done your affirmations, practice visualization and imagination exercises. Imaginations are powerful. Willpower without clarity and imagination is not as effective. So if you are going through chaos right now, don't despair. Through imagination you can transport yourself to a state of bliss. It has immense power to allow you to let go of your limitations and connect with universal energy. You move beyond the limits of your conscious mind and tap into the reserves of the subconscious mind, or sixth sense. How does that look to you? How does that feel? Hold onto that feeling; bring clarity to your imagination. Repeat it daily and often, and gradually it will become a reality. The *feeling* of having achieved Life Balance crystallizes the affirmation and imagination. If you create the feeling regularly, you make Life Balance a reality.

FEELING AND CONVICTION

When you feel your affirmations, you invite the universe to join you and help you achieve what you are seeking. The feeling begins with gratitude for and acknowledgment of what you've already received. After you write down your feelings, read what you've written and see whether it makes you feel good. For example, you might write: "I love knowing that my life is balanced and that I am spending enough time with my family, health, profession, and spirituality." Just reading this statement will energize you. The energy will increase the possibility of the outcome you envisioned. Your conviction will eliminate all doubts about the outcome and will keep your mind on what you want and away from what you don't want.

The legend of Babe Ruth's "called-shot" home run in the 1932 World Series dramatically illustrates the value of conviction. Playing in Chicago's Wrigley Field, the New York Yankees had won the first two games against the Chicago Cubs. They would go on to sweep the series four games to none. Ruth, the Yankees' top slugger, opened the game at Chicago's Wrigley Field with a first-inning home run, then came to the plate in the third inning. He took two strikes, and then, according to observers, pointed toward the centerfield bleachers. He knocked the next pitch over centerfield and out of the park.

Legend has it that a teammate asked Ruth, "What if you hadn't hit the home run?" Ruth's answer: "It never crossed my mind."

Where your attention goes, energy flows. Babe Ruth's philosophy was "Never let the fear of striking out get in your way." He didn't, and though he struck out more often that most players, he rewrote the record books when it came to home runs.

UNEXPECTED CHALLENGES

Unexpected challenges, enormous change, or pressing deadlines are very real and happen to all of us. The secret to surviving them is not to get ruffled but to maintain your equilibrium and enthusiasm and to stay centered. By relaxing and staying calm, you'll be able to handle things more effectively. Involve your family and your colleagues in these challenges. If they're with you, you won't feel alienated. They'll also help you overcome these challenges. Effective communication is the key.

There are times when you have to go through temporary imbalance. For example, as I write this, both of us are trying to complete this book while doing other necessary work. We thus decided to involve some of our family members and staff so they would feel that they were part of the project.

If the state of imbalance is temporary and short-term, it's OK to involve family and friends in this way, as long as they have bought into your project and are aware of your need to involve them. If this becomes a long-term problem, of course, you need to look closely and try to resolve it. Ultimately, enlightened persistence is displayed in the moment of choice.

How do you handle yourself when you are tested and challenged? How do you stick to your priorities when put to the test?

These are choices you make in a moment of integrity, and they determine your balance or imbalance. The more you exercise wise choices, the easier it is to continue to do so in the future. When you succumb to temptations you are less likely to withstand the real tests that are bound to come in life.

As you become successful, you face more challenges. With each success, the test gets bigger. As you overcome the first hurdle, a new one is put in its place. This is the universe's way of testing your capacity and ability to succeed. There is nothing wrong with this, since most of us never make use of our full potential. The key is to strive for balance as you tap into your genius. When life rewards your success with a bigger challenge, go for it, but be sure you keep your balance.

Make Life Balance you choice at every step of the way. If you have to choose between success and Life Balance, choose Life Balance. Success is empty without it.

TEMPORARY DEFEATS

"Pain is inevitable, suffering is optional," said the Dalai Lama, quoting an old Zen saying.

Life inevitably brings pain, even on the road to success. You'll encounter temporary defeats as you move toward your goals. Don't worry about them. Develop a good sense of humor; nothing is better for softening blows. Learn to laugh at yourself. When you see humor in embarrassing situations, they cease to be stressful. The person who can laugh often, and who finds humor in even the most stressful events, can keep going when others fail.

You can't win all the time. The great New York Yankees team of 1927 – the year Babe Ruth hit 60 home runs – lost 44 games. Michael Jordan, considered the greatest basketball player of all time, scored on fewer than half of his field goal attempts. Joe Montana, the Hall of Fame quarterback known for his passing accuracy and his ability to bring his team from behind, passed for more than 40,551 yards and 273 touchdowns during his National Football League career. But he also threw for 139 interceptions.

Great athletes know that they will fail often on their road to victory. They also know that every failure carries the seed of success.

"The ultimate measure of a man," said Martin Luther King Jr., "is not where he stands in moments of comfort, but where he stands at times of challenge and controversy."

In his younger days, Azim was not conscientious and didn't do well academically. In fact he did poorly in grade 12. His lackluster grades made it difficult for his uncle, who worked in the education department in Tanzania, to place him in a college in England. But once he was admitted to college, he did very well academically. In fact, he excelled in his studies and went on to gain three professional accounting degrees. So don't worry about temporary defeats. They're part and parcel of success.

Every failure makes room for future success, if you let every failure teach you a lesson. In a particular week, you may miss your one-on-one visits with your children, or you may have an argument with your spouse. You may have an important deadline, which puts all your plans on the shelf. This may make you lose hope and become fearful. You may think it's impossible to have Life Balance. This is fear creeping in and knocking at your door. Respond with faith and enlightened persistence, and it will go away.

Faith always wins over fear. A mother would never give birth to a child if she feared the pangs of childbirth. A bird would never take flight if it feared the unbounded sky. Respond to your temporary defeat by affirming that though this week did not go as planned, you still felt centered and balanced as you kept your principles and core values of family, health, and spirituality at the forefront. Enlightened persistence will make any setback temporary. But, to quote Tour de France champion Lance Armstrong, "Quitting is forever."

COURAGE

It takes courage to achieve Life Balance in the wake of a devastating defeat or extraordinary failure. But you can summon that courage if you believe in your capacity for balance. After experiencing the setback, don't retreat; take another step forward.

You won't achieve Life Balance by blaming others for your predicament. Take full responsibility, learn from every setback, keep your eye on the goal, and have faith in the outcome. This will begin an unstoppable journey to your desired outcome. You will persist as long as you believe. Belief creates enlightened persistence. When you take full responsibility, you take control of responses to your challenges.

If you don't believe in yourself no one else will. If you believe in yourself, others eventually will believe in you too. You have to decide your limits. You are the master of your destiny. You are also the master of your limitations. You set the bar, then let your inner capacity and the Universe do the rest.

Begin your journey now. Martin Luther King Jr. said: "Take the first step in faith. You do not have to see the whole staircase. Just take the first step." We build our castle one brick at a time. Little by little, we achieve our goals. We act small but think big. The tallest mountain is surmountable if we persist, day after day, in climbing it one step at a time.

Celebrate your small successes, and remember that all big things are accomplished by focused action and the discipline to follow through.

Be committed to your cause. Commitment means that your heart is in it. You want to achieve Life Balance. It really matters to you, and so you will give it all you have. It's like a signature on a contract: It binds you to a course of action. When a goal matters that much to you, you will find a way to accomplish it despite all obstacles and challenges. The power comes from within you. It's there and you may not even know it. With the knowing comes enlightened persistence.

TRUST AND FAITH

Recently, we have seen wars, technological revolution, recession, and the outbreak of Severe Acute Respiratory Syndrome (SARS). They all will pass, but other unpleasant events will follow. Life will continue to throw challenges at you. But you can respond to them with courage and trust. These qualities are the parents of persistence. We must remember that time acts definitely, but not swiftly. There are no quick fixes. Good things take time to happen, and things keep changing.

Have faith in what you do. This will pave the way for you to persist and get better at what you are doing. People who keep jumping from one thing to another seldom acquire balance. Enlightened Persistence requires that you stick to whatever path you have chosen and pursue it purposefully. If you dawdle when it comes to making decisions, you are showing lack of both confidence and foresight – qualities that are vital to success.

The principles of enlightened persistence have been demonstrated in the lives of great achievers such as inventor Thomas Edison, Kentucky Fried Chicken founder Harlan Sanders, IBM's Tom Watson, Chrysler's Lee Iacocca, and First Lady Eleanor Roosevelt. Men and women who excel in sports know the value of enlightened persistence. Ask Lance Armstrong, who, at last count, had won six consecutive Tours de France bicycle races despite his battle with cancer.

These same principles also apply in finding Life Balance. Nido and Azim both had imbalanced lives to begin with. Nido sweated 17 hours a day to put himself through school while adjusting to a new country and learning a new language. His confident persistence paid off as he passed his exams, built a business, and earned international respect as a businessman, speaker, consultant and educator. He also became successful as a husband and father. Although he always understood balance, it was not always easy to maintain it. But he got better at it through perseverance and experience, which led to wisdom.

Azim's story is similar. He eked out an existence as a student in England during the '70s, sharing a small apartment with five other students and eating Weetabix, the popular English whole-grain cereal, as his staple food. To pay his way through college, he cut up slaughtered chickens on a poultry farm by day and washed clothes at a laundry by night. By the time his daughter was born, Azim was busy building his professional accounting practice, volunteering on the Social Welfare Board in his community, and delivering motivational talks across the world. He lived an unbalanced life for about 10 years before he turned it around. He practiced visualization, affirmations, and imagination to help achieve a well-balanced life. He surmounted unexpected challenges and temporary defeats with courage, and accepted new challenges with trust and faith. He also budgeted his time, designing a pro-forma form for planning an ideal well-balanced week. He kept track of where he actually spent his time, and finally evaluated the variances and made the necessary changes for the next week.

As they write this book, both Nido and Azim believe they are leading well-balanced lives. They are grateful for the early struggles, which have enabled them to appreciate the beauty of living healthy, balanced lives.

They have demonstrated in this chapter that enlightened persistence is the key to forming the habits that constitute key ingredients in the achievement of Life Balance. Enlightened Persistence requires clarity, boldness, and commitment, along with the practicing of affirmations and visualization.

REFLECT ON THE FOLLOWING:

◙ Who brings home the treasure: the one who plunges deep into the sea or the one who stays at the edge of the surf?

◙ Think of a bird that fears the unbounded skies and has never flown.

◙ Think of a woman who fears birth pains and therefore has never given birth.

◙ Think of a caterpillar that goes into a cocoon and emerges as a butterfly.

◙ How do you go about climbing a mountain: In one leap or a step at a time?

◙ Do you get ruffled when you are faced with challenges?

◙ Are you willing to give whatever you have to get what you want?

◙ Do you know of a great person who never failed?

SUMMARY:

In summary, the transformation from imbalance to balance with Enlightened Persistence happens through the following steps:

◙ (1) Start with clarity. What does Life Balance mean to you? Write this down.

◙ (2) Visualize, affirm, and imagine your ideal status. Do this often. Feel the feeling.

◙ (3) Develop a joy for work. Choose work you love, or create love for the work you are doing.

▨ (4) Develop a passion and enthusiasm for whatever you do.

▨ (5) Anticipate obstacles and hurdles as you progress. Do not get ruffled or unbalanced because of them.

▨ (6) Learn from any setbacks and confront your fears. Write down what you learn so that it will crystallize in your mind.

▨ (7) March ahead despite your fears. This may sound reckless, but it's the way you make your fear gradually disappear.

▨ (8) Meet additional responsibilities without sacrificing your Life Balance and centeredness.

▨ (9) Be bold and committed. Commitment means you are in it for the long haul, and boldness has power.

▨ (10) Take small steps daily, one step at a time, to reach your goal of attaining Life Balance. Celebrate small successes.

▨ (11) Know that there are no quick fixes. Have trust and faith when progress takes time. Display Enlightened Persistence.

YOUR GOAL-SETTING EXERCISE
CHAPTER X: PRACTICING ENLIGHTENED PERSISTENCE

What areas in your life do you need to work on to practice enlightened persistence? Ask yourself: What one big obstacle is getting in the way of my working and living with enlightened persistence? Set your goal and timeline to overcome this obstacle.

My goal is to work on the following areas in terms of enlightened persistence:

....

....

....

I commit to the following timelines to implement this habit

....

....

....

If I follow through with this goal it will make a significant difference toward my balanced living.

GOAL-SETTING EXAMPLE:

Within the next 21 days I will articulate clearly what Life Balance means to me. I will act and behave daily as if I have already reached that status. I will pay particular attention to the feeling of achievement and balance.

"The oak sleeps in the acorn; the bird waits in the egg; and in the highest vision of the soul a waking angel stirs. Dreams are the seedlings of realities."

– James Allen

❋ ❋ ❋

CHAPTER 10

Mastering the Balancing Act

> *Doing too much or too little leads to failure.*
> — J. Paul Getty

QUESTIONS TO PONDER:

⊠ Do you feel that you are really living a life that is in balance?

⊠ Are you able to make the right choices naturally?

⊠ Do you have trouble deciding whether to follow your head or your heart?

⊠ Do you regard home and work as friends, or as enemies?

⊠ Do you enjoy healthy relationships?

⊠ Does your life revolve around the urgent, or around the important?

⊠ Would practical ideas on finding Life Balance be of help to you?

INTEGRATE THOUGHTS AND ACTIONS

Life is difficult. Many people rely on you: your boss, your colleagues, your customers, your spouse, your children, your parents and others. Their demands pull you in all directions, and you can't meet them all. It's often difficult to decide whom to gratify and whom to disappoint. The decisions require a delicate balancing act.

You can't perform this balancing act on pure instinct. Your decisions must be made consciously, and this requires an awareness of what you're doing and why you're doing it. Once you have learned to act consciously, your thoughts and your actions will become so integrated that you will make appropriate choices naturally, without agonizing over them.

Let's look at some areas of your life in which the balancing act is necessary, and at some strategies to help you make the appropriate choices.

MODERATION IS THE KEY

There's an apt expression that doubtless originated around the dirt tracks of Southern automobile racing: "He's got two speeds: wide open and stop."

The expression describes people whose inner drive compels them to go full-bore at everything until they achieve their objectives or collapse in exhaustion.

On the drag strip, it pays to go all out from start to finish. Staying ahead in the long run is not necessary because there *is* no long run; the race is over in a quarter of a mile. But when you're running the Daytona 500, wide-open is the loser's speed. If you try to go flat-out for the full 500 miles, you're likely to blow an engine before the race is over. The winner, in the long run, is the driver who strikes a balance between the fastest possible speed and the speed that puts the least stress on his vehicle. Winning the long race means adopting the fastest *sustainable* speed.

The principle applies in your life as well. Going all-out all the time in pursuit of every objective is a recipe for burn-out. To achieve Life Balance, it's necessary to pick your objectives and to pursue them at the optimum pace, which means the fastest sustainable pace.

It doesn't help to go at the fastest sustainable pace if you don't have a clear idea of where you're going. An airline pilot who picks up a tail wind, opens his throttle, and points his aircraft in the general direction of his intended destination may make excellent time. But when he arrives, he may find himself at the wrong airport.

A CLEAR VISION HELPS BALANCE YING AND YANG

To master the balancing act in life, you must have a clear vision and a commitment to make the vision a reality. You can't waste motion pursuing all the possibilities that are out there for you. You must decide which possibility you want to zero in on, and focus everything you do on this objective.

You must also understand all the aspects of your life, and keep them in balance. Taoists represent this as a balance between Ying and Yang. Ying and Yang represent the balance of opposites in the universe. When Ying and Yang are in balance, all is calm. When one outweighs the other, confusion and disarray set in.

Buddhism recommends the "middle path" – the one between the opposite extremes of luxury and hardship. Buddha believed that we all must take responsibility for ourselves and must practice self-control. The laws of the "Eightfold Path" were designed to guide people without making life too strict or too easy. They represented a "Middle Path" of living for Buddhists. They represent balance.

Staying in balance requires that you understand your whole being. You must know your physical, mental and spiritual needs, and you must bring them into congruence. If you don't understand how each contributes to the whole of your being, you may end up catering to one facet of your life at the expense of the whole. If you understand the whole in relation to its parts, you can determine the amount of time and effort to invest in each facet.

To acquire balance means to achieve that happy medium between the *minimum* and the *maximum* that represents your *optimum*. The minimum is the least you can get by with. The maximum is the most you're capable of. The optimum is the amount or degree of anything that is the most favorable toward the ends you desire.

Nido, in his book *Stairway to Success,* gives the example of the automobile. It may be capable of a maximum speed of more than 100 miles per hour, but if the end you desire is to have reliable, safe, and comfortable transportation, you'll never drive it at top speed. At 100 miles an hour, you'd be subjecting it to excessive wear and the likelihood of a fatal crash. At the other extreme, your car could crawl along at 5 to 10 miles per hour, minimizing the chances of your losing control on a curve, of crashing head-on into an object, or of rear-ending the vehicle ahead. But, at such speeds, your car would be highly inefficient as a means of transportation. It would be wasting time and horsepower, and if other traffic were traveling at normal freeway speeds, it would also be posing safety hazards.

Your car's optimum speed is a steady pace somewhere between those high and low speeds — probably between 60 and 70 miles per hour on an Interstate highway. That speed range usually provides the best combination of safety, fuel mileage, engine wear, and travel time.

Nido's *Stairway to Success* also points to the example of the Marathon runner who goes all-out for the first mile. This person will take an early lead, but the victory will go to the runner who strikes the highest *sustainable* pace. If your pace is too slow, the others will pass you. If it's too fast, you'll run out of energy before you reach the end of the race. You have to choose a happy medium.

You need to strike the same kind of balance in your personal habits and behavior. If at work you try to produce the maximum, you may face burnout. If you go for the minimum you will get poor results and will not tap into your potential.

Let us look at some aspects of your life that call for balance between Ying and Yang; that call for pursuing the "Middle Path"; that benefit from adopting the fastest *sustainable* pace.

HEAD VS. HEART

"Your reason and passion are the rudder and the sails of the seafaring soul," wrote Kahlil Gibran, the Lebanese-born philosopher, poet, and painter who wrote magnificently in both English and Arabic. "If either your sails or your rudder be broken, you can but toss and drift, or else be held at a standstill in mid-seas."

An equilibrium between reason and passion – between head and heart – is one of the essentials of Life Balance. It has been said that when the mind and the heart go to war, the body becomes the battlefield.

The mind allows us to think, to reason, and to apply our wisdom to make a difference. The heart is where we feel. Through it, we love and use our creativity without inhibition. When we merge education of the mind with education of the heart, we strike a dynamic balance. We look with "both eyes" – the eye of the heart and the eye of the mind. We look at life as a whole, realizing that one element affects the other.

The Dalai Lama, spiritual leader of the Tibetan people, explains that happiness comes from being balanced. He emphasizes that education without the balance of a warm heart can be dangerous and can bring unhappiness.

Jesus taught that happiness belonged to the meek, the merciful, and the peaceable. But in driving the moneychangers from the temple, he showed that these qualities must be balanced with boldness. Paul showed faith in this principle when he spoke of his gentle approach to dealing with the congregation but his boldness in dealing with its adversaries.

Bishop Desmond Tutu, the Nobel peace prize laureate and first black Anglican archbishop of Cape Town, South Africa, stresses the importance of a balance in our relationships with others.

"In our African language," he notes, "we say, 'a person is a person through other persons.' I would not know how to be a human being at all, except I learned this from other human beings. We are made for a delicate network of relationships, of interdependence. We are meant to complement each other.... not even the most powerful nation can be completely self-sufficient."

Reason without passion is lame, and passion without reason is blind. Reason alone is dull, whereas passion alone can lead to destruction. When we marry the two, we have a wonderful synergy. Our reasoning protects us from doing silly things. Our passion gives us the drive to excel and go the distance. Reason draws from the mind, passion from the heart.

HOME VS. CAREER

The balancing of home and career is the most common challenge executives face.

"No matter what rung of the corporate ladder you're on, constant vigilance is required lest demands eat up your home life," wrote Gay Hendricks and Kate Ludeman in *The Corporate Mystic.*

Many feel compelled to make a choice between home and career. Life Balance will make that stark choice unnecessary.

Technology was supposed to increase leisure time, presumably freeing us to spend more time with our families and less on the job. But technological progress seems to have brought us more things to do and less time in which to do them.

A study by Health Canada shows that almost 60% of Canadians who are employed outside the home cannot balance work and family demands. Most give higher priority to their work than they do to their families.

Flextime, which allows people the flexibility to schedule work time around family time, has been a major help in balancing family and work. Flextime, for example, might enable an employee to work 90% of a normal week for 90% of the pay. This could be enough to allow a parent to spend time with children after school. Flextime could also mean taking every other Friday off or working from home one day a week.

Flextime is especially helpful for double-duty mothers or fathers who frequently are victims of role overload. Life for them can be a daily grind of cooking and cleaning, supervising homework, driving children to school, looking after elderly parents, and running endless errands in addition to earning a living.

We're living now in the age of burn-out, in which workaholics pursue frenetic lifestyles that hog their time, drain their resources, and leave them empty and unfulfilled. Many people engage in activity for activity's sake, burying themselves in work or play to avoid facing real personal and spiritual needs.

Others are in love with money, and seek to express that love by spending all their waking hours pursuing their careers.

But truly successful people know that balance is essential to achievement, and they make room for quality time for family, friends, spiritual interests, and hobbies.

Lee Iacocca, as president of the Ford Division of Ford Motor Company and CEO of Chrysler, put in long days on the job. But he was also committed to staying home every weekend, enjoying time with his family, going to church, and reflecting on his life and times.

Nido and Azim both make it a point to schedule time with their families, even as their professional and civic duties multiply.

Nido spends 60 days a year on family vacations. He invites one member of the family on each of his business trips. Nido's eldest son, Ramsey, has been to 59 countries (38 of them with Nido). Nido also dedicates books to his family, one book per person; it creates a sense of importance. Nido has a toll-free number at home so that the children can keep in touch no matter where they are. Nido finds ways to teach his children at dinnertime, at fireside chats, and during walks on the beach. He has an agenda for nurturing in his children mindsets for success and significance.

Azim involves his wife and children in his work. Azim's wife does his creative writing. His daughter is one of his administrative assistants. His son is a "quotes" provider. Azim goes out with his wife twice a week, chips in with the household chores, and is a part of the team. He attends to the older parents living with him. Azim drops off and picks up his children from school regularly. He takes his children to all activities and watches their soccer games. He helps his son with his homework and coaches his daughter in soccer.

INDEPENDENCE VS. INTERDEPENDENCE

"No man is an island," wrote John Donne, 17th century English poet and churchman. We are all dependent on our fellow humans, and they are dependent on us. We are individuals with our own unique traits, but we are also tied to other individuals through bonds of family, religion, culture, community, nation, and many other commonalities. Our happiness depends to a large extent on how well we strike the balance between our independence as individuals and our interdependence with others.

When you foster strong and healthy relationships with others, especially those who are closest to you, the balancing act becomes easier. These healthy relationships provide a foundation for pursuing common goals. They also give you the confidence to pursue individual interests on your own. But if you don't cultivate healthy and strong relationships, achieving balance will always seem like an uphill battle. Strong, healthy relationships don't just happen. They require a huge investment of time and effort before they become reality.

Victoria Qubein, who was widowed when Nido was a small boy, gave her son an invaluable piece of advice: "If you want to be great, walk hand in hand and side by side with great people." Although she had only a fourth-grade education, she had a postgraduate's quota of common sense: Her advice helped Nido rise from a penniless state to the level of multimillionaire.

One of the most sadly neglected areas of interdependence is that between husband and wife. If you're married, the marital relationship must take priority over all other human relationships if you are to achieve Life Balance. Too many marriages have foundered on the shoals of indifference and neglect. All too many men and women, hard-pressed for time, have suddenly discovered that time has run out for the person at their side. After years of playing second fiddle to jobs, careers, hobbies and other activities; after too many evenings deprived of the company of a soulmate; after too many meals in which conversation was no deeper than "pass the salt," or "are you through with the Lifestyle section?" the marriage partner opts out, emotionally, physically, or both.

So don't miss a chance to take a pleasant walk with your wife, smelling the roses as you go. Don't miss an opportunity to take in a good movie with your husband. Look for shared experiences that will provide fuel for pleasant conversations far into the future.

Invest your time and heart in relationships with others who are close to you: your children, your extended family, your colleagues and your friends. Enhanced relationships lead to Life Balance and to joy in living.

The question of job vs. family doesn't need to be an either/or proposition. For example, one day Azim returned home late from work to find Tawfiq, his 8-year-old son, eager to play video games. Tawfiq was on a break from school and had been waiting all day for his dad to come home.

The next morning, Azim was scheduled to make an important business presentation before 40 senior executives. Should he disappoint Tawfiq and concentrate on polishing his presentation? Or should he use the evening to nurture his relationship with his son?

Azim chose to take Tawfiq to a video arcade. He later realized that the evening with his son was good for Tawfiq and good for business. It was a valuable chance to knit even closer the father/son relationship. And it took Azim's mind off business long enough for him to shed his stress and approach the presentation in a fresh and relaxed frame of mind. The presentation drew plaudits. Azim was a success at home and at work. It wasn't the result of good luck. It was the result of a good choice. It was the result of a balanced decision.

The balance between independence and interdependence has become critical in this age of diversity. Stephen Covey, in his book, *The 7 Habits of Highly Effective People,* explains that we are living in an age that values independence; yet we occupy a globe that is interconnected as it has never been before. This has created a massive imbalance. We all need to learn to make choices that lead us to invest time and effort in building trust, appreciating diversity, and valuing and respecting others.

Covey's advice: "Seek first to understand; then to be understood." What this means is that we must first seek to understand people who are different from us before we can expect them to understand us. Once we understand our own place in this interconnected world, we are better equipped to balance this interdependence with a healthy level of independence.

A healthy understanding of others is impossible unless you have a healthy understanding of yourself. Healthy independence requires a good relationship with yourself. A good relationship with yourself enables you to cultivate good relationships with others. It is an inside-out approach.

John Donne, whom we quoted earlier, compared the human race with the continent of Europe, and individuals with clods of dirt in his poem about the tolling of bells to announce the death of a parishioner.

"If a clod be washed away by the sea, Europe is the less," he wrote:

Each man's death diminishes me, For I am involved in mankind. Therefore, send not to know For whom the bell tolls, It tolls for thee.

Azim picks up on Donne's theme when he says: "We are all sharing the universe as one large family. When one is hurting we are all hurting. Oneness comes from realizing that we are all in the same journey even though we may take different paths to get there."

DO IT NOW VS. DO IT LATER

One of the songs sung at the funeral of the assassinated President William McKinley in 1901 was "Beautiful Isle of Somewhere." Written in 1897, it was about an imaginary land in which the sun was shining, the songbirds dwelled, and conditions were perfect. One of its verses begins this way:

Somewhere the day is longer, Somewhere the task is done...

Many people spend their lives dreaming about the "Isle of Somewhere" but never getting any closer to it. The isle remains indefinitely "somewhere"; the day is always "some day"; the accomplishment is always in the future.

Such people dream of taking that family vacation "some day"; of pursuing that hobby "some day"; of losing weight, or spending more time with their parents, or enjoying some other enjoyable experience in that misty "some day" on the "beautiful Isle of Somewhere."

It's time to stop postponing your dreams and your happiness. It's time to bring your beliefs and your actions into congruence. If what you do is not aligned with what you dream – if your actions are not aligned with your principles – then you're out of balance.

"Some day" is meaningless. "Today" is what counts. Sure, it's easy to let things slide; to put off bringing your life into balance. The worthwhile things in life require effort to acquire. But the rewards for persistence are sweet. Make the right choices today. Tomorrow, you'll be glad you did.

Life Balance manifests itself in many ways. It may be in the accomplishment of goals you set for yourself after leaving high school. It may be in the satisfaction that comes from the contributions you've made at work and in the security of having a retirement plan. You may achieve it through making friends or in cultivating outside interests such as the theater or sports. You may find it in a family life that suits your needs and standards. And you may find it in a set of ethics that you yourself have defined.

All these areas add up to the sum of your life. Look them over and decide whether you're satisfied with all of them. If you see areas where improvement is needed, go to work on them. Do it here and now. Don't wait until "some day" on the "Beautiful Isle of Somewhere."

BALANCE IN YOUR BUSINESS LIFE

Life Balance can bring richness to your personal life that goes far beyond the possession of material things, and significance to your business life that goes far beyond financial success.

Here are some things to consider as you seek balance in your business life:

SLOW VS. FAST

"Slow but sure wins the race," is the moral of Aesop's fable of the tortoise and the hare. "He who hesitates is lost," states the oft-quoted adage.

Life Balance requires a middle course between these two pieces of wisdom. President Theodore Roosevelt captured the idea in his motto: "Be sure you're right; then go ahead." The U.S. Supreme Court sought to establish such a course when it decreed that racial barriers in public education be dismantled "with all deliberate speed."

Doing things quickly can save you time, and that time may be spent doing more important things. But doing things in a rush, before you've had time to think through the repercussions, can land you quickly in the wrong place. Life Balance requires that you know what results you expect before you take action. It requires that you focus first on where you're going and how you plan to get there. It requires an assessment of obstacles and strategies for overcoming these obstacles. Only when you're focused on the destination, the ways, and the means is it advisable to proceed with all due speed.

TAKING RISKS VS. PLAYING IT SAFE

If you risk too much, you may lose everything. If you risk nothing, you will gain nothing. Taking risks is a balancing act. Intelligent risk-taking is a key to success in any endeavor. The baseball batter who stands at the plate and never takes the bat off his shoulder will never hit into a double play. Neither will he ever hit a home run. The best he can hope for is a base on balls. The worst he can expect is a strikeout. The batter who swings at the pitch is aware that the odds are against his hitting safely. The batter who hits safely 3 times out of 10 is considered a good hitter. Not since 1941 has any Major League batter hit safely better than 40% of the time over a season. But games and championships are won by players who swing at pitches, not by those who never go for the pitch.

How do you know when to take a risk and when to play it safe? Here's Nido's advice:

The process of risk analysis is not that complicated. Before embarking on a venture, answer these questions:

▨ (1) What is the best thing that could result from this action?

▨ (2) What is the worst that could result from this action?

▨ (3) What is the most likely result of this action?

If the *most likely* result would take you toward your vision, and you're willing to deal with the *worst possible* result in exchange for a shot at the *best possible* result, go ahead with the venture.

RETURN ON INVESTMENT VS. RISK

Return on investment is what you get from resources you invest. If you invest wisely, you're likely to get a favorable return. Investment is a complicated field in which you will need professional advice and require due diligence. People usually think of two types of return:

▨ (1) Return on investment (ROI), which is how much you get back in relation to the amount you invest.

▨ (2) Return on equity (ROE), which is how much a company earns in relation to the book value of its assets.

But even more important than these is your return on life (ROL). As Nido puts it, "ROL is what you get back from investing yourself."

Return on equity requires risk taking. The maxim is no risk no reward. Return on life is the return in joy and fulfillment you get from living your life fully. Return on investment and return on equity may be factors in your return on life. It depends on how you use them to improve the world around you. Nido offers this formula for securing a healthy return on life:

▨ Invest a third of your life in earning; you must *have* resources if you want to be able to *give* resources.

▨ Invest a third of your life in learning; read books and periodicals every week.

▨ Invest one-third of your life in giving and serving.

Nido also encourages his children to invest their money in different accounts. This teaches them fiscal literacy and also personal responsibility and accountability. Fiscal literacy enables them to build their futures. Personal responsibility teaches them to be accountable for their own destinies. And Nido's own example of giving time and resources to his community teaches them the value of investing for a healthy return on life.

Focus vs. Being Distracted

"For everything there is a season," wrote the wise King Solomon, "and a time for every purpose under heaven."

So when you've set aside time for a specific purpose, should you allow interruptions and distractions to break your focus?

Some people are easily distracted. They'll stop what they're doing at the drop of a hat and enter into an unrelated conversation, focus on a different train of thought, or embark on a different task. Others become so absorbed in what they're doing that they're oblivious of everything going on around them. It practically takes an explosion break their focus.

Life Balance enables you to know when to keep your focus and when to surrender to the distraction. If you allow yourself to be distracted by every minor interruption, every unplanned circumstance, you'll never accomplish anything constructive. But, as Solomon reminds us, there's "a time to keep silence and a time to speak."

Suppose your teenage daughter wants to talk to you heart to heart about a problem she's facing. Should you ignore her in favor of the column of figures you're adding up, the speech outline you're working on, or the specifications you're drawing up for an important project?

A few minutes invested in connecting with your daughter will, in the long run, more than compensate for a few minutes in which your business interests are put aside.

BALANCE IN YOUR PERSONAL LIFE

Balance in your personal life goes far beyond the accumulation of money and goods. At the end of the day, it's not how much you've enriched your material assets that counts; it's how much you've enriched your life, and through it, the lives of others.

How can Life Balance bring richness to your personal life? Here are some areas in which to cultivate balance:

RECEIVING VS. GIVING

It may surprise you to learn that it isn't enough to be a generous giver. Life Balance requires that you also be a gracious receiver. Giving and receiving are opposite sides of the same coin. For every gift there must be a receiver. If everybody gave and nobody received, to whom would we give?

There is joy in giving, so allow other people to give as well so they can also experience joy. When you perform as an artist and people applaud, allow them to finish their applause; people want to show their appreciation. Be worthy of both giving and receiving.

Kahlil Gibran explained the two-way benefits of giving and receiving this way:

...It is the pleasure of the bee to gather honey of the flower, but it is also the pleasure of the flower to yield its honey to the bee...and to both, bee and the flower, the giving and receiving of pleasure is a need and an ecstasy."

Less vs. More

You want to accomplish as much as you can. But when you aim strictly for volume, you may be adding accomplishments that add very little to your happiness or balance. Suppose someone were to show you a large bin containing a mixture of $100 bills and discarded tissue paper and offer to let you keep whatever you could remove in 30 seconds. Would you scoop up the contents by the handful, or would you quickly pick out the $100 bills and ignore the tissue paper?

You'd be most likely to go for the $100 bills, for they'd be far more valuable than the tissue paper. Picking up the tissue paper would simply distract you from picking up the important stuff.

In life, too, the best strategy is to focus on what is important and do it first. The person who does more is not always the person who succeeds. It's better to do a little that moves you toward your goals than to do a lot that gets you nowhere. And if an action moves you farther from your goals, it's best to heed the words of Lin Yutang, Chinese author and scholar who made the trek from Christianity to Buddhism and Taoism, then back to Christianity: "Besides the noble art of getting things done, there is the noble art of leaving things undone. The wisdom of life consists in the elimination of nonessentials."

Hard work vs. Laziness

A life of total leisure is the hardest career to pursue. But being overworked can cause stress and anxiety, which inhibit productivity. Life Balance means finding a middle ground between the two.

Quiet time can lead to ingenious ideas. A few moments spent in total relaxation can be more productive than hundreds of hours spent at hard labor. Archimedes, the ancient physicist and mechanical engineer, was given the task of determining whether a crown made for the king was of pure gold. The solution to the problem came to him as he lay in a bathtub. Archimedes reasoned that an object submerged in water would displace a volume of water equal to its own volume. By determining how much that same volume of gold would weigh, and comparing that weight with the weight of the crown, he could determine whether the crown was pure gold.

That bit of relaxation paid off for Archimedes. But if you spend all your time relaxing and meditating, your ideas will never make it out of your imagination. To implement your ideas, there's no substitute for hard work. So dream to bring your future into focus and act to bring it into reality.

Short-Term Imbalance

Once in a while it may be necessary to allow for temporary imbalance as a means to achieve long-term goals. Such imbalance is tolerable, and even desirable, if it is just for a short time. But if it continues long-term, it can lead to danger. An author working on a book may have to work extra-long hours to meet a deadline, or may have to go to extraordinary lengths to conduct research. Athletes training for the Olympics may have to push their bodies extra hard to whip them into shape for world-class competition. A contractor may have to push extra hard to bring a project in on time and avoid severe monetary penalties.

An occasional imbalance is OK if you're working toward something that will contribute to long-range stability. But make sure that the imbalance is temporary. And let your family and others close to you know what to expect.

MATERIAL RESPONSIBILITY VS. SPIRITUAL RESPONSIBILITY

At the end of the day we leave this world as we came – with nothing. So in the final analysis, material things become short-term and spiritual things long-term. But if we ignore our material responsibilities, we won't be able to sustain our spiritual side. So the balance between the two is important. In fact, if we were to marry the two it would be a good blend: pursuing material things with a spiritual foundation. We have multiple needs and we cannot ignore our spirituality by being obsessed with material well-being.

Azim has a friend, Naz, who once asked her mother how she would live her life if she were given a second chance. Her mother's reply demonstrated that material well-being was not her prime goal in life. She responded: "I would try to make twice as much difference in people's lives."

The Ultimate Aim: Well-Balanced Health

One of Jesus' parables concerns a prosperous farmer who filled his storehouses with grain and built new ones to hold more grain. Then he prepared to settle down for a life of leisure, telling himself, "Man, you have plenty of good things laid by, enough for many years: take life easy, eat, drink, and enjoy yourself." But God told him: "You fool, this very night you must surrender your life; you have made your money – who will get it now?"[9]

This man obviously was living an unbalanced life. He focused exclusively on his material wealth without thinking about his most important possession: life itself. In this modern world, where wealthy leisure is often held out as the ultimate goal, many individuals have stood at the pinnacle of success only to find themselves looking down into the grave.

Paul almost became one of them. He was a senior vice president of a major Corporation. He had been engrossed in climbing the corporate ladder, and was on the verge of realizing a lifelong dream: promotion to CEO.

Then he was hit by a series of distressing developments. First he learned that his teenage daughter had a drinking problem, apparently arising from her feeling that her parents were neglecting her. Then his doctor told him he suffered from a heart problem and would need an operation. Then he received a letter from his wife's lawyer. It was accompanied by separation papers. It caught him totally by surprise, though warning signs had been there for months. He had been so focused on his work that he had turned a totally blind eye toward his family and his health, and never realized it.

He recognized – just in time – that his life was out of balance and that success could not be sustained unless balance was restored. He made some conscious new choices, began putting his family and health first, and in two years had turned his life around.

---

[9] New English Bible (New York: Cambridge University Press 1970) Luke 12:20-21.

To accomplish this turnaround, Paul:

▣ Turned down the CEO position and opted to continue to work as senior vice president.

▣ Gave up part of his salary to hire an executive assistant to help him with his many administrative duties.

▣ Committed to build a friendship with his teenage daughter. He accepted her problem, showed her unconditional love, and scheduled regular weekly meetings with her.

▣ Went to counseling sessions with his wife to iron out their marital issues. He showed her that she mattered the most to him.

▣ Hired a personal trainer and worked with her three days a week. He also changed to a healthier diet.

Roger and Rebecca Merrill, in their insightful book, _Life Matters,_ use the term "navigational intelligence" to refer to the ability to make the choices that create what we want to have in our lives. Paul intelligently navigated his way back into Life Balance.

He began the balancing act as a reaction to his problems. If he had been proactive from the start, he might have avoided his heart condition, averted his daughter's drinking problem, and headed off his marital conflict before it became a crisis.

The good news is that no matter where you are in life, you can always make a fresh start. Where attention goes, energy flows. When Paul turned his attention toward his family and health situation, results changed – gradually but effectively.

SOME PRACTICAL TIPS

The Hour of Power

Azim, in his book, _The Corporate Sufi_, suggests: "Practice the 'hour of power' first thing in the morning: Twenty minutes of meditation. Twenty minutes of exercise. Twenty minutes of reading something inspiring. Go to sleep an hour earlier."

Starting your day with an hour of power gives you a head start. Generally, if you leave things for the end of the day, they don't get done. So we recommend that you start your day with things that are important in your life. For some disciplined people, exercising, reading and meditation in the evening works. If you are one of them and you have a good track record, then by all means continue. For others, early morning is a good time to start this habit.

Multi-tasking

Another way of finding balance is to combine two important activities. Try listening to educational CDs while driving or running on a treadmill. Or spend 20 minutes a day walking with your spouse, child or a colleague. That way, you make sure you are spending time with the people in your life who are important, and are still getting your exercise. By scheduling weekly family activities, exercise, reading, or prayer time, you can ensure that you do not overlook them in your busy week. Be organized and have good systems in place, to save time. Also, make good use of waiting time by reading and planning. Tackle your big goals a step at a time and they will become manageable.

"Undo list"

Eliminate unimportant elements from your life. If you can't eliminate them, delegate them. If you can't delegate them, postpone them. Then choose those remaining very important things in your life and execute them. In other words, execute around a tight set of priorities. Be proactive in putting important things in your life first.

LET PRINCIPLES, VALUES, AND ETHICS GUIDE YOU

Whatever you do, be guided by principles, values, and ethics and make appropriate choices that invite Life Balance. The key is to exercise integrity in the moment of choice; otherwise, everything becomes a theory with no practical application.

As you can see from the above, the balancing act is needed in many areas of life. Don't be overwhelmed by the many different possibilities. Focus on your vision and principles, and let them be the foundation for everything you do. Having a vision and keeping your feet on the ground will help you with the balancing act and will invite integrity and harmony into your life.

SUMMARY:

In summary you accomplish the balancing act by:

▨ (1) Knowing and articulating what balance means to you.

▨ (2) Understanding and writing down why Life Balance is important to you.

▨ (3) Knowing the various things you can balance. Some areas in which you can achieve balance include:

▧ Looking at home and work as friends. Involve your family in your work, and let them see how work helps home life.

▧ Building healthy relationships at work and at home. Invest time regularly to enhance this aspect that will greatly benefit Life Balance.

▧ Being efficient and effective. Don't compromise effectiveness for efficiency.

▧ Doing less. Focus on really important things in life. Avoid things that are not aligned with your goals and which do not significantly add to your success.

▧ Balancing your material and spiritual aspirations. Spend time to develop your spirituality – through reflection, prayers, and service to others.

▧ Striving for the optimum – not the minimum or maximum.

▧ Finding practical ways to schedule important things in your life. For example scheduling weekly time with your spouse, each of the children, and your parents. Scheduling time for reading, exercise, and meditation. Making time for reflection, journaling, and execution of work.

YOUR GOAL-SETTING EXERCISE

CHAPTER 10: BALANCING ACT

What are the areas in your life that you need to work on as far as the balancing act is concerned? Ask yourself: "What is the one big obstacle getting in the way of my doing the balancing act? Set your goal and timeline to overcome this obstacle.

My goal is to work on the following areas to help me make appropriate choices & do the balancing act:

....

....

....

I commit the following timelines to implement this habit

....

....

....

GOAL-SETTING EXAMPLE:

I want to give more to my family members:

⊠ *Spouse*

⊠ *Children*

⊠ *Parents*

⊠ *Siblings*

I commit to the following one-on-one weekly quality time together:

⊠ *Spouse* – Friday and Saturday evenings

⊠ *Daughter* – Sunday morning breakfast

⊠ *Son* – Sunday lunch

⊠ *Parents* – Sunday evening snack or dinner

⊠ *Siblings* – e-mail or phone call once a week

I will start this beginning this week. The only exception will be when I am traveling or if the family member I am supposed to meet is out of town.

> *When a mind stretches to embrace a new idea, it never shrinks back to its original dimension."*
>
> – Oliver Wendell Holmes Sr.

REVISITING *LIFE BALANCE IS YOUR CHOICE*

> *The greatest power that a person possesses is the power to choose."*
>
> – J. Martin Kohe

In this book we have asked a lot of questions and provided guidance on ways to get started toward Life Balance. If you have put our suggestions into action, you should be able to say "yes" to the following questions:

▓ Do you clearly understand what balance means to you?

▓ Are you able to master the balancing act amid chaos?

▓ Do you manage to stay balanced amid changes in your life?

▓ Do you live and work purposefully?

▓ Are you happy, upbeat, and performing at your peak?

▓ Have you been able to minimize your ego?

▓ Do you practice reflection and silence?

▓ Do you live, walk, and talk displaying excellence?

▓ Is your life contributing to yourself and to others?

▓ Are you well rounded?

▓ Do you manage your self and your time well?

▓ Do you display enlightened persistence to invite balance?

If you said "yes" to these questions, you are centered, you are anchored to your principles, and you have clarity of purpose. You have chosen Life Balance, and by so doing so have invited harmony and integrity into the frenzy of life.

You achieve Life Balance because you desire it and are willing to make the choices that invite it into your life. You choose to understand what Life Balance means to you, why it is important, and how you can achieve it. You commit to implementing what you've learned about achieving Life Balance. You make choices that lead to balance.

You realize that balance means different things to different people.

You understand that change is permanent and universal, and you adapt to it, using it as an opportunity to learn. But you hold firm to your principles despite all the change around. Change is a reality. Balance will not just happen amid all this change. You have to create it for yourself, and you do so by making appropriate choices.

You find practical ways to master the balancing act. You work from your center and find your optimum – not your maximum or your minimum. You have a strong bond with your household, which acts as an anchor and foundation upon which you build your working life. You find time to work hard, play, laugh, relax, and invest in healthy relationships.

You do the balancing act by an active process that requires your diligence, focus, and strategy. You don't just hope for an accident to bring about balance; you have a design.

You live purposefully at work and at home.

You set regular goals and think from your goals. These goals are aligned with your purpose. You are driven by results, not just processes. You focus on transformational activities and not transactional ones. You display authenticity, not just charisma, and seek a shared vision with the people in your family and with the people at work. You keep a healthy balance between your family life and your work life.

You keep the ego out of your system. You stay away from jealousy and defensiveness, which are ego-driven. You invite positive pride in lieu of those negative qualities. Thus, you keep your innate gifts alive and well. You are open-minded and non-judgmental, appreciating and valuing diversity. You have a strong self-image and self-esteem, and you invite love and harmony into your life.

You treat each day as a blessing and a gift, and cherish the beautiful life you have. You know that the destination is in the journey; thus you never cease to enjoy the ride. You practice stillness and meditation, which keeps you sharp and enhances your presence.

Silence and reflection bring you back to your center. When you are in your center, you are able to make wise decisions that are in harmony with your purpose. You are able to be spontaneous while following a planned course, and you are able to make both planning and spontaneity work for you.

You have a passion for excellence. You display excellence in everything you do: in the way you dress, how your office is maintained, how you deal with your staff. All your work and services reflect excellence; the way you do anything is the way you do everything.

You maintain healthy relationships and are a contributing member of your community. Whatever you do is a search and expression of your humanity and a way to contribute your energy to the world. You have moved from success to significance by making a positive difference. You are continually contributing to worthwhile causes – your family, colleagues, school, government, community, society, and self. Your contributions are made with love, respect, and humility. You are there when needed.

You take care of your health – physical, mental, emotional, financial, and spiritual. You manage not only your time but also yourself, so you do not let time manage you. You have achieved Life Balance by being holistic and not lopsided. You take proper care of yourself, not neglecting the things and people who mean the most to you. You have a sense of equilibrium, foundation and order. You are "running your car on all four tires."

Yes, there will be hurdles and challenges and obstacles and diversions, but you will remain steadfast, principle-centered, poised, and goal-orientated without ever forsaking your mission and vision.

Through your enlightened persistence, you'll be able to go the distance when things get rough and tough. You'll have the conviction that you will accomplish your goals, no matter what. With this determination, you go about achieving your goals and Life Balance.

For you, time is life and life is time. Your management of time means you are managing your life. You understand that life consists of a finite number of breaths. You realize that it's short and your longevity is not guaranteed. Thus, you live each day to the fullest, treating it as the most important day of your life.

You invite integrity and harmony into your life by maintaining equilibrium at the family, work, community, and global levels. You go about bringing harmony into your life by starting from yourself and transferring that integrity and harmony into all the other levels of your existence. You take the inside-out approach.

You are authentic and living in harmony with your true nature, doing what is right for you as an individual instead of trying to become someone else. You practice the different segments of integrity, including a wholeness of being and an unimpaired state of honesty, righteousness, honor, and virtue. These are all parts of integrity. You possess these qualities and can be trusted, because you are true to yourself.

You spend more of your time doing the things that bring you joy and satisfaction, thus inviting integrity and balance. Your body, mind, head, heart, and hands are in harmony. You have integrity, thus no conflict.

You walk and talk, eat and sleep, and go about your business, social, and spiritual exercises, making sure these facets of your life are integrated. You realize that Life Balance is your choice, and you have invited integrity and harmony into the frenzy of life.

You are integrated beyond the stages of being irritated with others and yourself. You are beyond the confines of bureaucracy and structure. You not only have insights, but you also have found congruence. Your walk, talk, actions, and reactions all reflect your mission. Everything in your life is poetry because your life is so synchronized. You see balance, feel it, and live it,

You say to yourself: "Today I begin a new life. Today is my birthday. I am born today. I am going to make the best of every day, every hour, every minute, and every second. I will grasp each moment and savor it – live it to the fullest. Never again is my life going to be the same; it will be exciting, energizing, loving, connected, opinionated, magnanimous, the best that God wished it.

"My life will be organized, methodical, visionary, planned yet spontaneous, focused, and going with the flow. Anyone who meets me will instantly be connected and feel my warmth, love, and authenticity. I will reflect what God's finest creation looks like. I have made the choice to invite Life Balance."

Life Balance is Your Choice. Make that choice. You can do it!

– Nido and Azim

AUTHORS' JOURNEYS: LIFE BALANCE LESSONS

NIDO QUBEIN'S JOURNEY

LESSON 1: The past does not equal the future (Enlightened persistence – Chapter V).

Nido spent his childhood in Lebanon, the birthplace of Kahlil Gibran, the great poet and writer.

As a child, he learned some wonderful Eastern values relating to family, humility, respect for elders, and community service.

Nido was just 3 years old when his father became ill, and 6 when he died. He grew up without the example and inspiration of a father, but his mother, Victoria Qubein, became a tower of strength for him, and he was determined to be a good father to his own children. As Mrs. Qubein put it, "Out of adversity beauty emerges." Relationships with family provide a strong sense of foundation for our emotional health.

LESSON 2: Pursuing Excellence (Chapter VII) comes from action.

At the age of 17, Nido left Lebanon for the United States with very little money and no command of English. He worked long hours in the beginning, studying for classes and working to pay tuition, room and board. He taught himself the language by learning 10 new words every day five days a week. Within a year, he had mastered English.

LESSON 3: Give and Receive (Balancing Act – Chapter I and Sense of Contribution – Chapter VII). Along his journey, Nido had some angels who helped.

First, there was his mother, who was a pillar in his life. She taught Nido principles you can't learn in school. Although she had only a fourth-grade education, she had a postgraduate's quota of common sense. She used to tell Nido: "If you want to be great, walk hand in hand and side by side with great people." Nido followed her advice and prospered.

At the end of Nido's sophomore year at Mount Olive College, he had saved $375 to buy a car. The price tag on the cheapest car was for $750. He was disappointed but not discouraged. He knew that he if he continued to save his money he could eventually buy a car. He related the story to his housemother, Verta Lawhon, who was a great listener. She received only $100 a month from Social Security and the college paid her $100 a month for her role as mother-in-residence. At the end of that month, Nido's bank statement showed that his balance was $750, even though he knew that it should have been only $375. He told Ms. Lawhon about it, thinking that perhaps the bankers didn't know how to add. Then it dawned on him: This woman, surviving on only $200 a month, had dipped into her paltry reserves and supplemented his bank account enough to swing the purchase of the car.

"I've decided it's much better for me to invest my money in the life of a budding young man than to park it in my savings account," she explained.

That was a huge turning point for Nido. It taught him that it is always better to give than to receive.

As Nido was finishing his sophomore year and getting ready to transfer to High Point University in High Point, North Carolina, the president of Mount Olive College told him that even though he had worked 10 hours a day, his earnings had been insufficient to pay all his school expenses. In fact, there was a big gap between the money he owed the school and the money he had already paid. But an anonymous doctor in a neighboring city had picked up the difference. Nido was so touched by the doctor's generosity that he wanted to meet him and personally thank him, but the doctor insisted on anonymity. Nido went to his dormitory room, knelt beside his bed, and made a commitment to God: When he began earning money, he too in some way would initiate a fund to help students go to college.

That was the birth of an idea. When he began his business in 1973, he acted on it. In the first year, he was able to give only one $500 scholarship. Today, the Nido Qubein Foundation awards about 50 scholarships annually for a total of about $200,000. Altogether, it has awarded about $3 million to 600 deserving students. Imagine what would happen if all 600 of these students were to commit similar acts of significance. In 2004, Nido was appointed president of High Point University. He took this position because he wanted to give even more.

When people ask Nido what areas of his life give him great joy, he always says that the Scholarship Foundation is a source of great satisfaction and significance for him.

LESSON 4: Meaning and satisfaction (Sense of Contribution – Chapter VII).

One of the things Nido has always done is to seek friends who are at least 20 or 30 years older than he. He looks upon them as sources of wisdom. If all you have is information, people will use you and then discard you. If what you have is knowledge, then people will need you occasionally. If what you have is wisdom, then people will respect you. Nido's friends had wisdom and they were willing to share it with him, thus becoming his heroes, models, and mentors. They gave him information and insight, and had a great impact on him. Some of them would tell him that they had invested their entire lives making money and ignoring their families, and how much they regretted that. Some said that they chose to make less money, and give their families quantity time as well as quality time. The irony is that the more they did that, the better equipped they became to deal with life's challenges and the more innovative they became in their businesses. As a result, they ended up still making significant fortunes.

LESSON 5: Caring for family, profession, service (Well Balanced Health – Chapter VIII).

Nido has climbed the ladder of personal and professional success. From a meager beginning as a penniless immigrant, he has become an internationally known professional speaker, consultant, and author.

Nido has been awarded many prestigious awards, including the Nido R. Qubein Philanthropy Award by the National Speakers Association, and the Philanthropist of the Year Award in his hometown of High Point. Nido is a partner in several companies and serves on the boards of 17 universities, corporations, and community organizations. He started the National Speakers' Association Foundation in Phoenix. He and his wife, Mariana, have four children. His business values, family values, and philanthropic endeavors represent a harmonious blend of Eastern and Western influences.

LESSON 6: If you believe you can make it (Enlightened Persistence – Chapter X).

Nido's success in America, from being a penniless immigrant to becoming a multi-millionaire, has been based on his faith that in America anybody who works hard and works smart can make it. He did both, and sure enough, his faith paid off.

LESSON 7: Create time for important things (Understanding the Time Myth – Chapter IX).

Good time management habits start at the top with the leaders at workplaces or institutions. But these habits don't automatically trickle down. They must be cultivated. Nido defines his capital as a sum of financial, educational, relational, and reputational capital. To build relational capital, he calls or writes to four clients a day. It's his way of connecting with people and staying in touch. He tries to have a good purpose for every call, and usually something of value to the caller each time.

It's amazing how many people Nido can reach in a

year, and how they feel that he cares about them because he calls them. In the same way, he has a list of 100 contacts. These are 100-plus clients or important prospects and leaders in circles of influence to whom he mails something every month. Again, it tends to brand him and position him in a way that creates maximum responsiveness and a very nice balance between business and life. The lesson here is to develop good habits and to follow through with them constantly and consistently.

LESSON 8: Fiscal responsibility (Well Balanced Health – Chapter VIII).

Nido has never given his children pocket money. They've had to earn it through good performance at school. And when their performance was unsatisfactory, they would owe Nido money. We should never reinforce behaviors we don't want to see repeated. The great thing is that the Qubein children normally made "A's" and went on to invest their money in the stock market. When it was their own hard-earned money, it had greater meaning to them, and they committed themselves to better planning.

Nido spends 60 days a year on family vacations. He invites one member of the family on each of his business trip. Ramsey, Nido's eldest son, has been to 59 countries (38 with Nido). Nido has also dedicated his books to his family, one book per person. This creates a sense of importance. Nido has a toll-free number at home so that his children can keep in touch no matter where they are. He finds ways to teach his children at dinnertime, in fireside chats, and during walks on the beach. He has an agenda to nurture and create a mindset for success and significance.

Nido encourages his children to invest their money in diverse accounts. He teaches them fiscal literacy so that they can compound their earnings and build their futures. He teaches them personal responsibility so that they assume responsibility for their own destinies.

LESSON 9: Spiritual and material responsibilities (Well Balanced Health – Chapter VIII).

Nido has a conventional will that details what happens to his material goods when he dies. That's simply a mechanical instrument, designed for maximum ingenuity in avoiding as much tax as possible. He lets a lawyer handle that. The one he spends his own time on is his ethical will.

He wrote a private document to each of his four children that says, "Material things come and go, but let me tell you what I've left for you that will stay with you all your years, and even more important, that you can pass on to many generations thereafter." This ethical will talks about values, about purpose, about character. This is a lesson in sense of purpose. It carries more meaning than raw figures.

AZIM JAMAL'S JOURNEY

LESSON 1: The past does not equal the future (Rejuvenating in Stillness and Presence – Chapter V).

Azim was born in Dar-es-Salaam (which means "Harbor of Peace) in Tanzania. In his early days in East Africa, Azim did not do well in his studies. He was convinced that he could not study. Azim was great at sports and excelled in soccer and cricket. He was used to coming home in the wee hours of the morning. In 1970 he went to Mombasa, Kenya, for two years, living in a hostel. The hostel doors closed at 6:00 p.m., and you couldn't get out after that. So Azim had to adjust.

LESSON 2: Meditation (Rejuvenating in Stillness and Presence – Chapter V) and service helps (Having a Sense of Contribution – Chapter VII).

In 1972 Azim began to meditate regularly from 4 a.m. to 5 a.m. He has kept it up for the past 32 years. The disciplined hostel life and the practice of meditation made Azim reflect on his lack of focus in his studies and his life.

He left East Africa in 1974 at the age of 17 to go to the United Kingdom to study for membership in Britain's Association of Certified Chartered Accountants.

In Britain, Azim was the stereotypical poor student. He lived frugally, sharing a small apartment with five other students. He lived on a cereal called Weetabix. It was cheap, healthy, and easy to prepare. He worked evenings during the college term and double shifts in summer, cutting up slaughtered chickens on a poultry farm by day and washing clothes in a laundry by night.

By the end of 1978, Azim had passed all his ACCA exams. In fact, he had passed 7 out of 8 of the exams in one sitting – a record for his college at that time. In January 1980, he migrated to Canada. Even with his professional accounting degree, it was a struggle to find a job. He slept on a couch at a friend's house for a few months until he landed a job and was on his feet.

The first thing Azim did after he got a job was to buy a car – a big, white Parisienne – the Canadian version of the Pontiac Catalina. He used it to give rides to elderly people, taking them to a church and running errands. They repaid him with prayers and good wishes. Azim believes that some of these prayers helped him in the hard journey from accounting for business to accounting for life.

LESSON 3: The past does not equal the future; the value of visualization, affirmations, imagination, and overcoming unexpected challenges and temporary defeats (Practicing Enlightened Persistence Chapter X). Time budgeting helps him live a balanced life (Understanding the Time Myth – Chapter IX).

When Azim's daughter was born, he was busy building his professional accounting practice, serving on the Social Welfare Board in his community, and making voluntary speeches across the world. He lived an unbalanced life for about 10 years before he turned it around for himself with visualization, affirmations, and imagination, and by overcoming unexpected challenges and temporary defeats.

He also budgeted his time to give his weeks ideal balance. He kept track of where he spent his time and evaluated the week-to-week variances to learn from his budgeting.

LESSON 4: Azim finds his Purpose (Chapter III) through silence and reflection (Rejuvenating in Stillness and Presence – Chapter V), when he was making a voluntary contribution (Having a Sense of Contribution - Chapter VII) in the third world.

Azim's defining moment came in 1997, while volunteering with Afghan refugees in Pakistan. Here, he shares his personal life-changing experience:

I was visiting a refugee camp where I met a family of 14 Afghan refugees living in one small room. I heard stories from people who had witnessed a father being murdered in front of their eyes. I was told of people who had walked barefoot for 18 days in the rugged mountains and of women who'd given birth in the wilderness. I was told how several of them, working 14 hours a day, couldn't make the equivalent of one dollar. Deeply moved by their plight, I sobbed like a baby during the cab ride back to the hotel. I went through a lot of soul-searching that night, and asked myself how I could help them. I was an accountant with three professional degrees, and I could surely afford to send some money every month, but nothing that would make a significant improvement on their dire condition. Besides, I was not passionate enough about accounting.

I wondered what I could do that would make me successful enough to make a significant difference to these people financially. Over the past 20 years I had been very successful in voluntary work, primarily in the area of motivational and inspirational speaking. Every time I spoke in this capacity, I discovered I had boundless energy and lost track of time. These engagements changed me. I learned so much about myself, about life, about purpose, and about others. One night, while I was in deep contemplation, the answer came to me. I was to become an inspirational speaker and author.

I decided that if I put my heart and my energy into it for 10 years, I could become one of the top 10 speakers in the world, able to sell at least 5.7 million copies of my books, and then I could help these people in a substantial way. It was a defining moment in my life!

LESSON 5: It is important to involve family in major decisions and to exercise a balance between reason and passion (Chapter II – Mastering the Balancing Act).

After discussing this change of career and getting the family blessing, I began withdrawing from the accounting firm in which I had been a partner since 1985. It was a gradual move from being part-time from October 1997 to October 2000 to becoming a full-time speaker and writer as of October 2000.

LESSON 6: Pursuing Excellence (Chapter VII) comes from action.

In 1999, I had 170 speaking engagements around the world and published my first book, *Seven Steps to Lasting Happiness.* I was unstoppable!

LESSON 7: Enlightened Persistence (Chapter X) and Ego – being open to the universe's message (Chapter IV).

Then, in 2000, I went through the darkest moment in my new career. Just before leaving for Great Britain to give a series of keynote speeches on lifelong learning, I stopped by a Vancouver bookstore to see whether my self-published book had arrived. My search on the store's computer by book title found no hits. Then I typed "Azim Jamal," and was confronted by the message, "Author Unknown." That was my lowest point; I felt I had made a mistake. I had let down my family. I had put all my money and thousands of hours of my time into this business, and I couldn't find my book in the bookstore.

Filled with self-doubt, I was leaving the store when I spotted a book titled *The Greatest Salesman in the World,* by Og Mandino. I almost walked out, but was drawn to the book by some magnetic connection. I picked it up and, flipping to the introduction, read how Mandino, an aspiring author, had been on the verge of suicide after he went broke, and his wife and children had walked out on him. But he managed to turn his life around through positive thinking, and went on to sell more than 30 million books. I was inspired!

To me, that was a message from the universe telling me that if Og could do it, I could do it. When I was almost at wits' end, the inspiration came. Through openness and perseverance, a path was shown.

I have never looked back since then. I am the author of several books including *The Corporate Sufi* and the best-seller *Seven Steps to Lasting Happiness.* I am an expert on Life Balance and have spoken to more than a million people worldwide in organizations and corporations of varying sizes. I have received rave reviews and testimonials for my books from many world-renowned authors, including Deepak Chopra, and I am co-authoring a book with a legend – Nido Qubein!

LESSON 8: Life is a journey, not a destination.

The big question remains: Have I realized my dream?

From one perspective the answer is. "Absolutely not!" We never quite arrive. Throughout our lives, we aspire to reach new goals; therefore, we really arrive only when we die.

From another perspective, the answer is a

resounding "Yes!" I am doing what I love doing; I am really passionate about my work, losing track of time when I am engrossed in it. I travel around the world speaking frequently, speaking to diverse audiences. I have the full support of my spouse, the blessings of my parents, and children who cheer me on. Moreover, I am making a difference every day to others and to myself. I am doing what I had promised to do when I was born. If I were to die today, I would have no regrets. In this sense, I have definitely arrived.

FAQ

Q. WHAT DOES LIFE BALANCE MEAN?

Life balance can be viewed.in many ways. It can be a balance between home and work. Or a balance among body, mind, and soul. Or it may be a balance between one's material and spiritual lives. Life balance is a state of feeling and being. You know intuitively that you are doing the right things, and you're able to navigate through the many opportunities and challenges, keeping in mind the priority and importance of living a balanced life. You know what is important to you, and you are able to choose appropriately.

Life Balance can be achieved by spending enough quality and quantity of time in important areas of your life. Strive to feel connected to your center amid change and chaos.

Life balance is not a static condition. It is a dynamic and evolving blend of the body, mind and spirit. It is important to know what Life Balance means to you. To know this, you need to know what areas of your life are the most important to you.

What's the big deal about balance?

With balance you don't get burned out, and you are thus able to sustain your success. Also, you find meaning and fulfillment when your life is balanced. You feel calm and happy, not stressed and frustrated.

When is the best time to do the right things?

If you wait for the right time to do right you may never get around to it. The time is always right to do the right things.

What makes you who you are?

As we choose, so we are. If you want Life Balance, make wise choices that lead you to Life Balance.

How does a busy corporate person become balanced?

One way to achieve this is to become a "Corporate Mystic." Mystics are interested in the essence, not the form. They look at what's inside, not what's outside. They are not concerned with outward appearance of others: how they look, the clothes they wear, the cars they drive, the houses they live in, and the money they have. To the mystic, these things matter little. It is what's inside people, – their character and spirit – that interests the mystic. Corporate Mystics are people who marry their work with their life missions and balance their work, family, social, and spiritual lives. They are ambitious and want to do well in the worldly sense of climbing the corporate ladder, raising families, and being materially successful, without compromising ethics and principles. The Corporate Mystic is one who walks the mystic path to spirituality with practical feet.

Does Life Balance mean being balanced at all times?

No. There will be times when you will be

unbalanced. As long as these periods are temporary and short-lived you are OK. If these periods become the norm, you need to worry about it.

Does balance mean giving up your career and success?

No. It means inviting success into your career. Balance leads to long-term success.

How do I balance my life with so many multifaceted demands?

Start by identifying things that are very important in your life. Eliminate or postpone the less important items. If you focus on doing things that are very important, you'll find that your time is well utilized, allowing you to balance your life. Try keeping track of where you spend your time for a week and then ask yourself how much of the time was spent on things that were really important to you? This will be a very revealing exercise, and will help you take steps to achieve balance.

Why am I exhausted, yet underutilized?

This situation means you're spending your energy in areas you have no business being in. This is sure to lead to imbalance.

Why is it that many people don't live to their potential?

They don't find their purpose in life or a worthwhile cause to contribute to. You tap into your genius when you find your calling and create a desire to make a difference in a worthwhile cause.

If you lack clarity in what you want or don't know why you want it, you won't be able to live to your potential. You also need conviction to accomplish the things you want to achieve in life. Finally, lack of action and discipline to execute your goals can keep you from living to your potential. For you to realize your potential, you must have faith when you are faced with obstacles and challenges.

When you live to your potential, you are content with yourself. This feeling helps in inviting Life Balance.

How can I know what my calling is?

Go back into your past to recall when you felt you were at your best. What were you doing at that time? Why were you so excited? If you won a lottery of $40 million, what kind of work would you do? If you were to die today, what is the one regret you would have? These responses will help reveal to you what your gifts and calling are. This clarity helps in achieving Life Balance, because you are able to focus on what you want.

How do I know I am doing the right thing in my personal and work life?

Listen to the voice inside you. Only you can hear it. Trust that voice! It will be your best ally and guide. Being in alignment with your conscience is important for feeling balanced, too.

Why does it seem easier to meet a difficult professional demand than to meet an easy emotional need in a relationship?

This is because you have not realized that emotional issues need as much energy and attention as professional issues; therefore, you shortchange your efforts in your relationships. When you do so, you feel frustrated and unbalanced.

How do I get out of my boring routine and create enthusiasm and vigor for my life and work?

Routine and structure have their merit. However, becoming a slave to routine and structure can be counterproductive. To create enthusiasm and vigor for your life and work, you need invigorating goals. Also, the "whys" behind the goals have to be energizing and meaningful. Set a goal for achieving Life Balance.

Is it possible to live to your potential and have Life Balance as well?

Yes, you can have them both. Find your calling, connect it to a worthwhile cause, and put the bulk of your energies into it. By having this focus, you let go of the things that do not connect, or only marginally connect, to your purpose. This process of getting things undone leads to Life Balance.

What does ego have to do with balance and potential?

Ego creates negative energy. It makes you defensive so that you take things personally. This takes away the energy that you could use to realize your potential. With negative energy around, you sway away from Life Balance.

Describe the power of love.

A house built through the power of love will last an eternity, but a house built with the finest materials but with the power of love lacking may not last a lifetime.

When there is love, there is God, and with love your life becomes a work of art, a piece of poetry. Love transforms your life the way a caterpillar is transformed into a butterfly. You let the subject disappear in the object. You realize you have been created and are not the creator. You no longer take things personally, become defensive, or harbor suspicions. No more complexes – inferior or superior. No more boundaries or turf wars. No more edging gifts out. Love invites balance; ego edges it out.

Why is being defensive counter-productive?

If you became defensive, you exert a lot of energy, which is counter -productive. When you go into acceptance, you defuse the situation and let resentments disappear. Defensiveness invites imbalance. Open-mindedness invites balance.

If you are good from within, does it matter what others think?

Don't worry about what others think. Focus on being true to yourself. Other people's opinions do not change who you really are.

How do I become present and live in the moment?

Treat each day as the most important day of your life. Further, think of your breath as a priceless gift. No breath, no life. By being conscious of our breath, we suddenly become present. Also, say to yourself that no matter at what stage you are in life, you can be happy only in the moment; you can't be happy yesterday or tomorrow. Think of the basketball player having a second to go and needing two points to win. He needs to get results *now*. His opportunity lies in the moment, not in the future or the past.

Remember always that we create our tomorrows through the work we do today. Being present and living in the moment invites Life Balance.

How do I remove clutter from my mind?

Go into silence. Practicing meditation and spending time near nature enables you to remove clutter from your mind and paves the way for creativity and intuition. A peaceful mind really helps you to feel balanced.

By concentrating on the moment, your mind steers toward the most important thing in the moment at the exclusion of everything else.

Why are we so consumed with the past and with the future?

The ego doesn't want to forget past failures or hurts. It doesn't want to let go of the baggage. It loves to dwell upon it. It derives its importance from it. The ego also has a tendency to worry about the unpredictable future simply to avoid the present moment.

What can we really say is ours?

The six feet of land that we will be buried under is all that is really ours. We can take nothing else, physical or material, along with us to our graves.

Why do you say that it is easier to be excellent?

It may seem hard to believe that it is easier to be excellent than to be mediocre. But the reality is that when you're excellent, you feel good about your work, your team feels good, your customers feel good, and your rewards are good; therefore, there are no comebacks, complaints or frustrations. All this creates a positive energy chain. The reverse is true when you do work that is below par. When you make excellence a habit, you want to be excellent in balanced living as well.

Why does excellent work create momentum and success?

Half-hearted work is counterproductive because you have to repeat what you have done. You are not happy doing the work. When you do your work wholeheartedly. there is gusto and enthusiasm, which creates momentum and success. If you go about achieving Life Balance wholeheartedly, you have a far better chance of achieving it than you do if you go about it half-heartedly.

Whose life is the most noble?

The ones who make the most difference to their fellow creatures have lived the noblest lives. When you make a difference to your near and dear ones, you say hello to Life Balance.

How do I keep my composure when really tested by a very difficult person?

Difficult people come into our lives to teach us something. Ask yourself what you are learning here. If you are getting frustrated, ask where the frustration is coming from. Is it coming from the other person or from your reaction to the other person? Ask yourself whether you're taking things too personally. If you are, why are you? Once you address this, you will have a far better chance not only of keeping your composure but also of coming out richer each time this happens. This way you can keep your balance even when tested by difficult people.

How important are your relationships?

Within your relationships you experience your real growth. Also, it is not what you have, but who you have in your life that counts.

What is a key to healthy relationships with close ones?

Trust! Accepting the words and feelings of your partner at face value and without judgment is the key. By showing complete trust, you validate both your partner and your relationship. Also, schedule time with each other for communication or relaxation. Show utmost respect at all times, even during trying times. If the other party is being unreasonable, continue your respect and love, thereby shifting the other person's attitude. If we treat other people as if they were what we want them to be, they will generally lean toward becoming what we want them to be. Avoid the blame game. Instead, take it as a learning game. Healthy relationships are an important ingredient of Life Balance.

Why does achieving Life Balance take a long time?

It is an irony of life that you value most what is most difficult to get. When you look back at your success, what do you remember most? Not your success, but the hard times you had to go through to get that success. Why? It's because that is what you cherish the most – the feeling of accomplishment, of having surmounted all the difficulties to win the prize.

Why do we need to go through struggle to enjoy what we have?

If you don't work for your success, it's very hard to

value it. Value comes from the sweat you put into your success. Easy come, easy go, is the way it works. When you earn your success, you cherish it. This is a wonderfully fair concept.

Why are there so many obstacles en route to Life Balance?

Obstacles allow you to tap into your genius. No obstacles, and you will be a weakling, never tested, never growing.

Why is imagination more powerful than willpower?

Imagination has no limits. Your imagination takes you to the land of possibilities. Willpower without imagination is limited. The key to success is to imagine vividly the picture of success and frequently to implant this picture in your conscious and unconscious mind. This should be followed by focusing all energy and attention on achieving the success you've imagined. This process is more powerful than just willpower. If you can vividly imagine Life Balance, you can invite it.

Why is life so complicated?

Life isn't complicated unless we make it complicated. The great truths in life are simple. Therefore seek simplicity in complexity. Simplicity attracts balance; complexity attracts imbalance.

How do I recover from a loss or hurt in love?

Realize that your soul has opened and you are on fertile ground for spiritual growth. If you take this as a positive, you became open to incredible growth and vast possibilities. Some of the best books are written by people who have lost in love.

How can I be happy in good times and bad times?

Good and bad times are cycles of life. They are only temporary. Realize that when night is here, day is not far away. When spring is here, winter is not far away. When sorrow is here, joy is not far away. You can have Life Balance in good and bad times -- no matter what.

How do I translate my vision into daily action?

Break down your long-term vision into many goals and break down your goals into many activities. Schedule these activities in your weekly and daily plans. These daily actions create a momentum toward your vision. Effective execution of your goals creates Life Balance.

What should you do when you are faced with obstacles and adversity?

Embrace your difficulties and maintain an upbeat mood. Send the message to the world that you are going to make it, no matter what. Keep persisting and become unstoppable. This attitude is contagious and can be extended to the achievement of Life Balance.

The Universe seems unfair – why do some have plenty while others have nothing?

The Universe is fair: It gives you what you create in your thoughts and what you believe and work for. Not everyone wants to be rich and famous, even though that might sound surprising. Many are scared of success and feel they will lose their privacy. Some believe they are destined to fail. Yet some find solace in telling others that they have nothing. Yes, there are many situations, especially in the Third World, where there are dire, genuine problems. There are things that you have control over, and there are other things that you don't control. You can't control natural disasters, or prevent death and old age. What you can do is to cultivate healthy habits so as to have the best chance of living a long, healthy life. You can also control your reactions and attitudes when faced with challenges and problems. You can be proactive and prevent problems that are preventable. When you follow these steps you will find that the universe is being fair to you.

Do thoughts create your destiny?

Yes, your thoughts are like nourishment to your being. As you nourish yourself with upbeat, positive thoughts, you invite positive results. They are the starting points for action.

You may have heard the saying: "Sow a thought and reap an action. Sow an action and reap a character. Sow a character and reap a destiny."

Thoughts are the seedlings of your destiny. Sow a thought today about enjoying a balanced life. Thoughts lead to choices, and appropriate choices invite Life Balance!